PICTURING THE ROSE

PICTURING THE ROSE

A Way of Looking at Fairy Tales

MARCIA LANE

THE H.W. WILSON COMPANY / 1994

Printed in the United States of America
First Printing   #28495787

Library of Congress Cataloging-in-Publication Data

Lane, Marcia.
    Picturing the rose : a way of looking at fairy tales /
by Marcia Lane.
      p.   cm.
   Includes bibliographical references and index.
   ISBN 0-8242-0848-X
   1. Fairy tales—History and criticism.   2. Fairy tales—
Classification.   I. Title.
GR550.L32   1993
398.21—dc20   93-5777

There, nestled in the petals of a wild rose,
was a tiny babe.

Jane Yolen from "The Rosechild"
in *The Moon Ribbon and Other Tales*

CONTENTS

ACKNOWLEDGMENTS

This book would never have been written if not for the help and support of a number of people. I wish to thank my friend and editor, Judy O'Malley for suggesting the book in the first place. I owe a debt of gratitude to many storytellers, especially Mary Hamilton, Hughes Moir, and Margaret Read MacDonald, all of whom read, and by reading, improved this book, and Jane Yolen, who kindly allowed me to quote from her tale "Rosechild," which expresses the central image of this book. I am especially grateful to Michael Burke and Nancy Petaja, whose endless good humor, love, and forebearance have seen me through this and many other projects. And I am finally able to thank Lynn Passy, who knew I could write a book even before I knew it.

The author is grateful to the publishers of the following works for permission to quote selections:

The European Folktale: Form and Nature by Max Lüthi. Tr. by Jon Erickson. Copyright © 1976 Indiana University Press. Used with permission of Continuum Publishing Company.

The Fairytale as Art Form and Portrait of Man by Max Lüthi. Tr. by John D. Niles. Copyright © 1986 Indiana University Press. Used with permission of Continuum Publishing Company.

The Hard Facts of the Grimms' Fairy Tales by Maria Tatar. Copyright © 1987 by Princeton University Press. Used by permission of publisher.

Implicit Meanings by Mary Douglas. Copyright © 1978. Used by permission of Routledge & Kegan Paul.

Have you ever read a fairy tale and thought, "Well, that's interesting, but I don't understand"? Or, better yet, "I loved (or hated) that story, but I don't know why!" Have you ever wanted to research the elements of a story, but found the huge volumes of commentary daunting? This feeling of inadequacy is reinforced by the disdain, conscious or not, which anthropologists seem to feel for those storytellers who tell primarily for children. As storyteller and collector Anne Pellowski writes in her preface to *The World of Storytelling* (H. W. Wilson Co., 1990), "To my dismay, I realized that folklorists, in general, have a very poor opinion of story compilers and storytellers for children. They criticize them for poor scholarship, for watering down and changing original stories, and for the artificial manner in which they learn and tell stories." The first time I tried to read Marie-Louise von Franz's *Feminine in Fairy Tales*, I got through about twenty pages before I realized that I had only understood (or *thought* that I understood) the first two paragraphs of the introduction. I was in a state of despair, thinking, "I'll never be fit to tell these stories, because I can't understand von Franz!" Then it occurred to me that before there was a Marie-Louise von Franz, there was a storyteller, just like me.

At about the same time that I came to this somewhat obvious revelation, I had the good fortune to hear Gioia Timpanelli talk about her own path as a storyteller, and about Italian and Sicilian stories. The kinds of connections she drew—between the spoken word and painting, sculpture, music, religion, history, and geography—opened my eyes to possibilities I had not, until then, explored. When I started thinking about fairy tales as *accumulated experience*, not just narration, then many other links became possible. I began to think about how fairy tales connected to different aspects of everyday life—chores, relationships, child rearing, etc.—and to the other activities of the imagination—fantasizing, singing, wishing, fearing, aspiring!

If I say to you, "Think of a rose," your mind conjures up a picture of a flower—but your picture is unique. You imagine a new, tight bud, or a full-blown flower. Everyone sees a different rose. Take it by the stem and rotate it slowly and, second by second, it transforms right before your eyes. Each time you look at it, it's different, but the rose is still there. In much the same way, fairy tales tend to change as we live with them, examine them, and tell them. Return to the rose. Close your eyes and the perfume will resurrect the image of the flower. Always the same, always changing. These stories will blossom as you examine them; you can look and look, and they will never lose their ability to delight and enchant. Such is their power!

This book is an attempt to balance the scales, to give storytellers greater confidence in their own abilities and intuitions (backed up with a little hard information). This is a "user-friendly" reference book. Read what you need, add to my suggestions or invent your own methods—whatever will increase your comfort level as a storyteller! And, in the process, you'll gain an entry-level understanding of some of the "scientific" theoretical approaches to thinking about fairy tales.

The practice of taking fairy tales seriously as literature probably started in the seventeenth century, with collections of folklore in Italy (*The Pentamerone*, by Giambattista Basile) and France (*Contes de ma Mere l'Oye*, by Charles Perrault and *Contes des Fées*, by the Countess d'Aulnoy). There followed English translations of collections of stories from India (*The Panchatantra* and *The Mahabarata*) and the Middle East (*The Arabian Nights' Entertainments*). By the time Jacob and Wilhelm Grimm came along in the early nineteenth century, there was an established tradition of collecting the stories of the "common folks." There was also a growing practice of scrutinizing those stories to discover what lessons, messages, and values they were transmitting. Early folklorists (although they were called "students of popular antiquities"!) believed that folktales were reformulated remnants of ancient myths. They saw a kind of cosmology in the struggle of the hero (force of light, sun, day) over the villain (darkness, night). So, even early in the evolution of the study of folklore, there was an awareness of motifs that were common to stories from widely differing cultures.

By the turn of the century there was increasing interest in a psycho-analytic approach to understanding folktales. According to Freud and his disciples, the "solar hero" was symbolic of the phallus, and the night was the all-protecting, all-devouring womb. C. G. Jung (and, later, Joseph Campbell) took another tack, and saw archetypal symbols of a collective consciousness and unconsciousness, life and death, in the struggles of fairy-tale characters.

The rejection of psychoanalytic approaches to folklore led to structuralism—the attempt to find a consistent and predictable grammar, like the structure of a sentence, in folktales. The Russian scholar and writer Vladimir Propp applied this theory to a number of the stories in the Afanas'ev collection of Russian fairy tales in his book, *The Morphology of the Folktale*. Propp took the different episodes of the story, and showed how the same basic components could be organized in only a certain number of combinations. This was in 1928, only eighteen years after Antti Aarne had published (in Finnish) the first catalog of tale types. Another kind of structural analysis was developed by the French anthropologist, Claude Levi-Strauss. He proposed a way of analyzing the structure of myths to understand how different cultures expressed the same concepts of group or individual development.

Ever since the phenomenon of the Disney-animated fairy tales (beginning in the 1930s), the widespread acceptance of television in the 1950s, and the advent of computers and the Space Age, the study of fairy tales has revolved around their effect, deleterious or not, on children. In the 1950s, virtually everyone thought that television would result in the equalization of education. If everyone could afford TV, then every child would have the same access to information and educational programming. And fairy tales? Well, in a generation that was involved to the point of obsession with the idea of space travel and clean, never-ending nuclear power, fairy tales were considered "unscientific." It's important to realize that the first Disney films were considered a refreshing return to fantasy. Despite the current feeling that Walt Disney bastardized and trivialized these very potent stories, for their time, the Disney films were quite daring—they dared to be unrealistic! They dared to be unscientific, and just plain entertaining.

In recent years storytellers (among others) have come to realize that fairy tales, like myths, have far-reaching consequences for adults as well. But we continue to look at these stories from limited perspectives. If you are of a Freudian bent, then Bruno Bettleheim's very forceful (if sometimes misguided) examination of fairy tales, *The Uses of Enchantment*, decodes the stories in one particular fashion. The viewpoint of Jung's collective unconscious is reflected in his own writings, and in those of Maria-Louise von Franz and Joseph Campbell. And a gender/political awareness is the focus of Jack Zipes's book of modern literary fairy tales, *Don't Bet on the Prince*, and of many contemporary fairy tale studies. Constructionalists, deconstructionalists, feminists, social historians, and psychologists have all taken a crack at the parsing of the fairy tale.

For the two categories of people who matter most, all the books amount to linguistic excess. Simply put, kids don't care about, and storytellers can't use most of what has been written about fairy tales. For all the theorizing that has gone forth about the nature of story, and the ability of a child to perceive and internalize various aspects of story, the truth is, no one can be really sure. Even our adult recollections of listening to fairy tales as a child are colored by years and experience, and by the need to assign meaning to events and artifacts of our youth.

For us as storytellers the challenge is to approach fairy tales with an openness that allows each story to speak to us, and through us, with many voices. To that end, I have taken information and material from several different sources—some scholarly, others more folksy—and attempted to consolidate them into a unified approach to fairy tale-telling. In doing so, my goal is not to validate or invalidate any of the wonderful and scholarly work that has been done on this subject, but rather to create a method for using Freudian, Jungian, gender-based, historical/sociological/geographic, and *intuitive* ways of looking at the language of fairy tales. My feeling is that some or all of these insights may be appropriate for different stories, but that the educated intuition of the teller is always essential. It seems obvious to me that in any art-form (and I believe that storytelling is an art, separate from but related to writing and acting) there is enormous subjectivity, and no single answer to the question, "What does it mean?" could possibly be valid for everyone.

This book is divided into two sections: Part I examines different aspects of fairy tales—style of language, characters, plots, predictable outcomes, etc. This section serves as a basis for the "story-work" that gives the teller better ways of learning and enlarging on the stories. Part II is a collection of some of the stories that I tell. In each case I've given the reader the text of the story as I tell it, followed by a description of the kind of work that I did in order to make informed choices in the telling. I have included some excerpts from non-Western fairy tales, specifically Native American and African. I do tell stories from these traditions, but I feel that it is extremely important for the teller to do as much exploration into the *cultural* aspects of these stories as into the language and the structure. Even though I use the same methods and some of the same reference books, I feel less than secure making pronouncements about stories that come from cultures that are less familiar to me. I still tell these stories, but I constantly remind myself that I cannot possibly know all of the connotations they contain (see Part I, Chapter 2).

In those places in the text of Part I where I give examples of particular stories, I have tried to take them from easily accessible sources. It would be impossible to cover every aspect, every facet of fairy-tale literature, but it is my hope that this book will serve as a springboard for those who want to delve deeper, and as an overview for those who don't. One doesn't have to look to the most obscure fairy tales in order to see patterns and situations that are common and identifiable. And it doesn't take a scholar, toiling away among dusty tomes, to find stories that will keep you—and your listeners—charmed and engaged for a lifetime!

PART I

Aspects of Fairy Tales

CHAPTER 1

Where Is the "Fairy"?

> Fairy: A term loosely used to denote a type of supernatural being, usually invisible, sometimes benevolent and helpful, sometimes evil and dangerous, sometimes just mischievous and whimsical, dwelling on the earth in close contact with man.
>
> from *Funk & Wagnalls Standard Dictionary of Folklore, Mythology, and Legend*. Harper & Row, 1984.

Do you remember the first fairy tale you ever heard? Probably not. The very first fairy tale you ever heard probably went into your brain, rattled around for a while, disrupted a few neurons, and departed. But it left its mark on your ability to perceive certain implications about time and space and gender and many other facets of life and language.

In time you heard many other fairy tales. Some you liked and asked for over and over again, and some you hated on first hearing! Some were promptly dismissed. But with each additional tale, you gained a certain level of understanding of these issues: real versus symbolic, here versus somewhere, possible versus "im-". We form a picture of inner and outer life through an understanding, not only of the stories we are hearing, but also which types of stories.

With the exception of literary fairy tales (a genre that has only really been recognized since the stories of the early nineteenth century), all orally transmitted fairy tales are folktales, but not all folktales are fairy tales. By that I mean that all of those stories come from an oral tradition,

1

but not all satisfy the requirements—anybody's requirements—for fairy tales. The exact definition of "fairy tale" has been a matter of debate for a long time. Even the "experts" agree that, for a story to qualify as a traditional fairy tale, it must contain certain elements, but they don't all agree on what those elements are. There may be a supernatural or magical being, a sort of "fairy substitute," if you will! Therefore, stories with genies, ogres, imps, wizards, brownies, witches, sorcerers, oni, or fairies are all fairy tales. Beyond that stipulation, however, it all falls apart. Some writers on the subject firmly believe that if there is no supernatural being, then there is no fairy tale. Others feel that any magical occurrence fills the bill. You might say that a talking animal is a magical creature, but in many common European folktales (and in Native American and African stories) the animals talk up a storm, and the effect is one of ordinariness, not magic. Perhaps it is safe to say that a talking animal is only remarkable when the story chooses to remark on it. "The King, however, had a lion which was a wondrous animal, for he knew all concealed and secret things." So, in the Grimms' fairy tale "The Twelve Huntsmen," the story itself tells us that the lion is magical, not because he can speak, but because he has a special vision. He can see the truth.

There are other issues involved in classifying fairy tales. It is generally accepted that if a story is represented as having happened to a real person (living or dead) then it qualifies as a legend—no matter how magical the events in the story. Likewise, if a story happens at a particular time (that is, "in 1492," for example) then it may be history or legend or lie, but it is usually not fairy tale. Issues of time may, indeed, be magical. In the classic Japanese fairy tale "Urashima" the hero spends three nights under the sea, and when he returns to land he finds that three hundred years have passed. The Washington Irving story "Rip Van Winkle" employs the same device, but in this case we know the author, so folklorists and storytellers generally regard this as a literary legend, and not one from the oral tradition. That holds true even though Irving may have used many of the local Catskill traditional oral legends in the body of the story.

Another measure of oral story versus literary is the presence of a distinctive "author's voice." This is, at one end of the spectrum, fairly obvious. For example, it's obvious that the language in "Rip Van Winkle" is the creation of a specific nineteenth-century author, and therefore not characteristic of a fairy tale. It is highly stylized, and not a product of the oral tradition. "In the High and Far-Off Times the Elephant, O Best Beloved, . . . ," is an opening phrase that marks a story as one of Rudyard Kipling's *Just So Stories*. On the other hand, there are gifted story-writers who choose to hide (or, at least, soften) the evidence of single authorship. Jane Yolen, Richard Kennedy, Eleanor Farjeon, and Alan Garner are just a few examples of contemporary writers whose works have a timeless, classic feel to them.

The task of making hard and fast decisions about what is or is not a fairy tale has become more difficult and complex as the lines between oral and literary have blurred. Most of the literary stories of seventeenth-century author Charles Perrault were oral fairy tales before he wrote them down, and are definitely considered "classic" fairy tales now. But C. Perrault is still in the picture! After all, like the Grimm brothers, Perrault did write, and by writing, codify those stories that we modern tellers adapt, adopt, and tell. He also edited, arranged, and selected the stories. All in all, it is getting harder and harder to separate the folk from the author in most story collections that purport to be "pure."

Even in cases where there are no magical occurrences, no chatty animals, no ogres, there may still be a fairy tale! The story that happens in a place that is more of the mind than of the map—that is a fairy tale. In *Hard Facts of the Grimms' Fairy Tales* (Princeton Univ. Pr. 1987), Maria Tatar describes a continuum from folklore (oral literature) to literature (the written-down variety). Then she plots an intersecting line that runs between naturalistic and supernaturalistic settings (see diagram p. 4). Tatar describes fairy tales as stories that occur in supernatural settings, and may be either oral or written literature. Folktales are defined as those stories that happen in naturalistic settings and, again, may be either oral or written. According to Tatar, the Grimms' stories fall into all four quadrants, depending on the nature of the story, and on how much creative rewriting was done between the original source and the published version.

If you think about the opening "lines" of a story, any story, you can see that genre usually reveals itself in the first moments of the telling. "In the beginning . . ." —no matter what is said after that moment, this story has marked itself as a myth. Other traditional "myth-markers" would be

Naturalistic
Setting

Oral Folktales   Literary Folktales

Jack and the King's Daughter (U.S.)   When Schlemeil Went to Warsaw
                                                                  (I.B. Singer)
The Boy Who Went to the North Wind
(Norway)   The Rootabaga Stories (Carl Sandburg)

How Frog Got Long Legs (Ghana)

Folklore   Literature

Oral Fairy Tales   Literary Fairy Tales

Rapunzel   The Girl Who Cried Flowers (Yolen)
The Twelve Huntsmen   The Caliph Stork (Hauptmann)
Urashima   The Water of Life (Pyle)

Supernaturalistic
Setting

Note: Based on a diagram by Maria Tatar with story titles added by author

"Once, in the beginning of days . . ." or "Before people were made. . . ." Personal stories refer to the teller, as in, "When my father was ten, he got his first pet, a pug dog." Obviously, no matter how much rewriting has gone into this tale, it comes from a particular perspective, a personal historical reference. "There was once a farmer and his wife, and they were forever arguing about who had the harder job." There, in one sentence, is a folktale! Now, if the story goes on to describe a test of wills, silly accidents, reconciliation, then it is a common, garden-variety folktale. If, however, an imp comes out of the sugar bowl and creates havoc, or if the husband catches a golden fish that begs for its life, then you have a fairy tale.

My own definition of fairy tale goes something like this: A fairy tale is a story—literary or folk—that has a sense of the numinous, the feeling or sensation of the supernatural or the mysterious. But, and this is crucial, it is a story that happens in the past tense, and a story that is not tied to any specifics. If it happens "at the beginning of the world," then it is a myth. A story that names a specific "real" person is a legend (even if it contains a magical occurrence). A story that happens in the future is a fantasy. Fairy tales are sometimes spiritual, but never religious.

It may be cold comfort to the novice teller, but the truth is that after reading and telling dozens of stories you will find that a true fairy tale, like gold, tends to make its presence felt. And, like class, although undefinable, everyone knows it when they see it!

CHAPTER 2

The Basket Is Not the Fruit

Every spoken sentence rests on unspoken knowledge for some of its meaning. Some speech contains most of its meaning in verbal form. Some carries very little. This is the essence of the distinction . . . between two speech codes: the one attempts to elaborate all its meanings verbally, the other relies heavily on context.

from *Implicit Meanings—Essays in Anthropology* by Mary Douglas. Routledge & Kegan Paul, Ltd., 1975.

The folk tale is the primer of the picture-language of the soul. Joseph Campbell in the commentary to *The Complete Grimm's Fairy Tales*, Pantheon, 1944.

If you think about it for a moment, you can see that language is symbol. That is, the word for a thing, and the thing that that word indicates are different. When we say "chair" we are using a commonly understood English-language indicator for a particular item. We have utilized that particular indicator for so many years that it almost seems synonymous with the object. But imagine a situation where you walk into a room that has no recognizable chair; maybe a room filled with cardboard boxes and stacks of books. If someone were to walk into that room and say to you, "Won't you take a chair?" you would probably look around, find a box or stack of a convenient height, and sit down. You have reinterpreted the word "chair" to mean "object to keep my fanny off the floor," and you have made the necessary adjustments.

In looking at various kinds of stories, we constantly make the mistake of assuming that the words are the story. Storytellers have frequently heard the same question from so many non-tellers: "How do you memorize all those words?" And most tellers will patiently explain what every teller knows—that we don't memorize. Tellers each have their own way of describing the process, but the one aspect that is shared by all those descriptions is the idea of vision, of seeing a path or route or pattern in the story.

What we understand instinctively (if there are enough years of experience to back it up) is that the words we say are not the story, but rather an indicator for the story. If you think of a bucket of water, you can clearly see that the bucket is not the water. The bucket is the container, the thing that makes it possible to transport the water. Without the bucket (or some other container) you would find it nearly impossible to "have" water, but they are not the same thing.

The concept is even more obvious when you imagine a strong, clear-nylon net and some fish. The net may be almost invisible. You can see the fish, touch the fish, even smell the fish, but the net is still there. The container is not the thing contained, no matter how closely they coexist.

The same thing is true of all speech. The words we use are conventional indicators. They carry the meaning, but they are not the thing itself. That's what gives language its enormous flexibility. We can use the exact same words but make them mean different things, depending on the situation, the person addressed, even our mood. Words are a kind of code, and they can give us a great deal of information above and beyond the concrete, the denoted meaning. But that depends on our being able to break the code. Even in common speech words carry political implications, sexual implications, a whole range of connotative values. When we are dealing with the language of story, and especially of fairy tale, words also take on the burden of conveying a heightened sense of significance. The word "cloak" may denote an article of clothing, but the connotations include "hide," "obscure," "pretext," and "protection," to name a few.

When words are joined together to form phrases and sentences and whole stories, the levels of meaning are multiplied. A word that means one thing at the beginning of a story may mean something very different at the end. Uncovering those possibilities (not certainties, for stories are not carved in stone, no matter what strict traditionalists may say), is the mission of the serious teller of fairy tales. We pry into these stories, not to de-mystify them, for such a thing could never happen, but to look at the range of potential meanings within the words, to make us more alive, conscious, and vibrant tellers. We examine the words in order to tell them, perhaps blithely and without outward dramatics, but with the sense of security and comfort that comes from living with them. But even here, the feeling is that the more we live with these stories, the more we realize their special nature. They are like the cat we've had for years—such a good, familiar friend, but still another species!

The decoding of story language is part science, part art. In the first aspect, we can use the standard tools. Dictionaries, encyclopedias, and thesauruses, particularly *The Oxford English Dictionary*, which gives antiquated as well as current meanings of words, are excellent primary resources for tellers. It is remarkable how many would-be storytellers don't even consider the possibility of multiple word meanings. Another obvious (though sometimes unavailable) source of information in the case of stories from languages other than your own, is an alternate translation. In the case of Grimms' fairy tales, there are numerous translations to choose from. Of course, not every translation is "honest." That is, translators, like tellers, frequently edit or rearrange the stories. Or, quite innocently, a translator can simply miss a meaning or mistake a connotation. The best we can hope for, barring a friendly neighborhood linguist, is to do the most complete possible investigation of library collections.

The artistry of language decoding lies as much in experience of life as it does in storytelling experience. In any storytelling experience, the frame of reference of the listener is as much an issue as that of the teller. There is an anecdote about a minister who preached a sermon on the evils of drink. He knew that some of his congregants didn't feel that his sermons were very memorable, so in order to give his lesson added impact, he planned a little practical demonstration. He took two glasses, one filled with water and one with alcohol, and showed them to his flock. Then he took a worm and dropped it into the glass of water. The worm wiggled around a bit, then swam to the side of the glass and crawled out. Then the minister dropped the same worm into the glass of alcohol, whereupon the worm thrashed about, curled into a ball and died! The minister turned to his congregation and asked, "Now, what have we learned from this?" A little boy in the front row spoke up. "If you drink alcohol, you won't get worms!" It is virtually impossible (and certainly ill-advised) to control what the listener *hears* when the teller speaks. Even if the teller and the listener are of the same cultural group (so they start with the same understanding of implied meanings), the differences in personal experience guarantee that each listener will form particular— and sometimes radically dissimilar—images from the teller's words.

It is a much-quoted truism that each time you tell a story you learn something new. That's undoubtedly true, but even this learning demands more than a mere rote recitation of the story. In one sense it is necessary to become so conversant with the fairy tale that you can tell it and listen to it at the same time. The result is that certain words and phrases begin to rise above the rest of the text, and take on greater importance. The traditional language of stories provides access to those varied meanings. Those phrases which are, to adults who have heard the stories over and over again, cliches, are actually talismans to remind the listener that the real meaning lies below the surface of the words. It then becomes possible to explore that language with the tools mentioned above, and with the additional tool of subjective impression. There is no guideline for this exploration. There is no beginning or end to it either. It is the action that keeps the story alive.

CHAPTER 3

Out of Space, Out of Time

> The fairy tale conquers time by ignoring it.
> from *Once Upon a Time: On the Nature of Fairy Tales* by Max Lüthi.
> Indiana University Press, 1976.

The first way in which the language of fairy tales differs from that of other folktales, of myths or legends, and of common speech (that is to say, speech which exists for the purpose of conveying information), is how it deals with time and place. Simply put, the traditional openings of fairy tales all work to inform the reader/listener that the story is not about the here and now. "Once upon a time, in a kingdom far away," " In a place, neither near nor far, and a time, neither now nor then," "Once there was and was not," "Long, long ago, when stones were soft," all these classic openings set a tone for the story that follows. They constitute both a disclaimer (don't worry about these things, they are not of your time and place) and an enabler (anything is possible, because the events that follow are not bound by the laws of the real world that we know). So, the first thing that language tells us about fairy tales is that they happen within an inner landscape. They belong to a place that is far removed from the plebeian concerns of reality, the physical world, and yet that is familiar to everyone. The stories happen, quite literally, in the country of the mind and of the heart.

Have you ever stopped in the middle of a fairy tale, and asked a child,

"And what do you think happened next?" Nine times out of ten, the listener will come up with a completely appropriate scenario. It might be outrageous or even directly counter to the rules of our physical world, but nevertheless it will be in agreement with the possibilities of the story. The child has internalized the rules of this other world, and can create a logical step in the sequence. Once we make a decision to go "long ago and far away," we are able to accept all the consequences of that decision. Animals can talk (if we say they can), shoes are magically able to leap buildings, a drink of water can change you into a beast, the hedgehog is a prince in disguise. This is not to imply that anything can happen. As teacher and storyteller Hughes Moir notes, every event, ordinary and extraordinary, "must conform to, and contribute to building, a fragile imaginary world that is temporarily believable." All this is possible, even expected, because we are in no-time, no-space.

So, one of the first clues that fairy tales have to offer of their meanings is any mention of time. There are magic and symbolic combinations: three days and three nights, one week, seven years, twelve moons (the use of the moon's cycle as a temporal indicator is frequently used to indicate the female nature of one aspect of the story), quick as a wink—all are significant cultural markers. They may link to seasonal images for some listeners, the number twelve indicating the months of the year. For some they may evoke menstrual cycle or migratory patterns. In some cultures, the celebrations of certain rites of passage go on for a week. However, as Max Lüthi notes, "Narrow and rigid interpretations cannot be ascribed to a dynamic story. . . . One must guard against the desire to interpret every single feature, every thorn and every fly" (*Once Upon a Time*, 33).

The no-space element is often invoked to give the listener the sense that the events of the story happened just out of range. "In a town just over the northern hills" may have given peasant listeners the feeling that strange things could happen outside of the protected walls and meadows of their valley. In some stories the message seems to be, "Stay here! Here you are safe. Out there demons abound!" On the other hand some stories say, "You must journey in order to become more than you are!" In fairy tales, the latter far outnumber the former. Fairy tales acknowledge that true growth demands a kind of travel—not necessarily in geographical terms, but travel in psychic distance—in order to become a wiser, more

terms of height or depth. The symbolism of going into the earth or up to the highest mountaintop is not really obscure. After all, humans (or, at least, those in Western cultures) have, for millenia, looked upward to the gods, and downward to the "dark forces" of the universe. We define divinity as being unreachably high. The conceit that evil (or the unexplainable and frightening) is within the earth, below our feet, may come from ancient explanations of earthquakes and volcanoes, but it is just as easily understood as an expression of inner conflict, suppressed anger, or sexual drives. There is very little science involved here. It is a matter of which psychological theory (or mix of psychological, anthropological, and theological theories) you choose to adopt for a particular story. The "cave-as-womb" may work for one tale; another one might suggest "cave-as-belly-of-the-beast."

Human beings, perhaps as a function of our curiosity, need to hear the end of a story; we crave closure in the events and relationships of our lives. Similarly, it is vital—particularly when dealing with anything as potent as the fairy realm—to settle one's business with that world before returning to this one. The power of fairy tales lies, at least partly, in the ability they possess to bring us face-to-face with frightening and magical creatures and events. For a child, the possibility that those creatures might spill over into the everyday world is the source of bad dreams and unresolved conflicts. For this reason, and to give a feeling of "roundness" to the story, there must be an act of closure, a spell of binding at the end. Just as "once upon a time" is the incantation that opens the gate to the fairy-tale world, there must be a similar incantation, that closes it.

In many western European stories the popular ending is "and they lived happily ever after." Others include, "and if they are not dead, then they're there still," or "and they feasted for seven days and seven nights. I was there, so I know!" The ending utilized in some Italian stories is "They had a great feast, and here we are with nothing!" Whatever those words might be, they serve to seal off the story world from the "real" one. It is not only a good, satisfying ending for a storytelling experience, but also a protective device for children who might otherwise find it difficult to detach from the story. The words are like a marker: that world, those people and places, they are not now. They do not have the power to harm.

Our goal, as tellers, is not to exactly re-create the political world or the geographic location in which the story was originally born (even if it were possible to know), nor to create a "new" interpretation of the story. Our goal is to recognize all the ways in which the geography of story language affects us, the ways in which it affects the listeners, and then to get out of the way of those images!

CHAPTER 4

Who Are These People?

> The fairy tale takes its heroes from the remotest branches of
> society: the prince and the young swineherd, the despised youngest
> son or the clumsy boy; and the girl who watches the hearth or tends
> the geese and the princess.
>
> from *Once Upon a Time: On the Nature of Fairy Tales* by Max Lüthi.
> Indiana University Press, 1976.

In fairy tales, as in life, there are only three ways to uncover the characters' essential natures. You can tell who they are by what they say about themselves, by what others say about them, and by what they do. Character is revealed by the choices we make.

Invariably, the world of the fairy tale is inhabited by a certain kind of royalty. "There was once a king and queen who had no children." Or, "One time there was a princess who refused to marry." Frequently the royals are balanced by peasants. The coming together of rich and poor, or haves and have-nots, is a common theme of fairy tales. By defining a character as royal, the story gives that character a certain flexibility of behavior that is outside the norm for the story-listener. The audience is able to believe that a king may decide (as in Perrault's "Donkey-Skin") to marry his own daughter, and there is nothing anyone can do to stop him. Royalty transcends the limitations and the constraints of the common folk: poverty, ignorance, class, law. On the other hand, a king may have distinct obligations—to marry a certain princess, to fulfill a promise, to follow the dictates of his country's traditions and his position. In addition, there may be degrees of royalty that dictate what a character may or may not do. The king of a poor country is at the mercy of a richer or stronger king. A prince may be royal-born, but he is constrained by tradition, and is generally limited in power. Historically, a princess had even less flexibility than a commoner! She may never have been allowed to travel alone, and she was at the mercy of her parents (notably, of course, her father), and even her own maids! In the very complex story, "The Girl Who Banished Seven Brothers" (*Arab Folktales*, Pantheon, 1986), a young girl is sent off to retrieve her brothers from a distant land. Her mother provides her with a camel to ride, and two servants to insure that she arrives safely at her destination. But the manservant forces her to change places with the maidservant. They rub pitch onto her skin, to reinforce the image that she is of low birth, but when she meets her brothers, and helps to groom them, her tears fall on her arm and dissolve the pitch, revealing the deception.

In numerous tales the princess is promised or bartered to another royal family, to become the bride of a prince who is not her choice. These stories most certainly reflect the political reality of the day, and in fact "real" princesses probably rarely managed to alter their fates, as fairy-tale princesses do! "Maid Maleen" (Grimm, #198) spends seven years imprisoned in a tower because of her love for a prince who is unacceptable to her father. When the time finally comes for her to be set free, she realizes that no one will free her, so she frees herself, only to find that the prince, believing her dead, is to marry another, an "ugly princess." She presents herself at the castle, and the ugly princess forces Maid Maleen to stand in for her at the wedding. But as she goes toward the church, Maid Maleen sings to the nettles by the side of the road (and to the sea, and to the church door) "Nettles stand aside, I am the true bride." That night, the ugly one takes her place in the bridal bed, but when the prince asks her about the songs she had sung, she denies them, and the switch is revealed. Maid Maleen regains her proper place, and the story provides resolution. True nobility is recognized.

The nature of nobility, in fairy tales, lies not in birthrights, but in intangibles. A kind and generous spirit, a sense of honor and duty, the ability to transcend physical limitations (for example, to wear out three pairs of iron shoes in search of one's lover) are the true marks of aristocracy. For more examples, see "East of the Sun, West of the Moon," "The Black Bull of Norroway," and "White Bear Whittington," all of which involve a long quest by the heroine before she can regain her husband.

In the classic fairy tales, characters frequently are nameless. Or if they have names, those names are designations of a quality or talent or secret that the characters possess. The princess may be "Bellissima," or "Rose Red," but these are more accurately descriptions rather than proper names. The same is true of the commoners. "There was once a miller who had a wife." Through the rest of the story, these two will be referred to as Miller and Miller's Wife. They are Everyman. In medieval days they would have been easily recognizable to the listeners. Their lives are defined by their jobs, and the fact that the fairy tale presents them with some magical offspring ("Hans, My Hedgehog") or some remarkable adventure might explain part of the appeal that these stories have held for "commoners" like us through the ages. If the Miller's daughter can outsmart the little man who spins straw into gold, if she has the courage, then she might become the Queen. If the poor Vassilissa can remember her dead mother's words of advice, and be kind to all she meets, then she may come home with a basket full of gold. Whether these lessons actually translate into actions that assist us in real life is open for debate! If fairy tales only feed dreams, then they serve us poorly. But if they empower children (and adults) to behave nobly in everyday situations, if we can use our wits as an alternative to brute force, then fairy tales can give us options for solving problems.

Of all the many characters who are the mainstay of fairy tales, the most prevalent are the Three Siblings. They may be the three sons of a poor farmer, or the three princesses of the king, or the three daughters of the merchant, whatever the case, there are certain characteristics that will be true of all of them. The youngest child will invariably be the parent's favorite! The youngest child is frequently the "fool of the world," neither the strongest nor the smartest, but she will inevitably succeed where the others fail. In some stories the youngest child will have to overcome not only the trials and tasks of the story, but also the animosity and deceits of the older siblings.

These stories make a great deal of common sense, when you consider the legal and social positions of youngest children. In European countries most inherited wealth went to the eldest male child. Younger sons might get a portion of land, but more often they would be taught a trade and left to fend for themselves. The oldest daughter would be first in line for a good marriage. The youngest daughter might be relegated to spinster status, kept at home to care for aging parents. If she had a brother, he would be responsible for maintaining her upon the death of the parents. If not, then she would inherit whatever land and/or property there was, but these would be her dowery if and when she married. Consequently, an older spinster would have been either a burden or a "catch," depending on whether or not she had brothers. It stands to reason that stories that portrayed the adventures and triumphs of youngest children would have been very popular! They are our surrogates, the Davids who triumph over countless Goliaths!

The heroes of fairy tales are virtuous and/or clever, kind and brave, honest and, most of all, lucky! In fact, one classic fairy tale is called "The Luck Child" or, in some versions "The Child of Fortune." The element of luck is one that the poorest story-listener could understand. Some people simply seem to be born under a lucky star or sign. Perhaps it is easier to accept disasters if they are matters of destiny, and cannot be called your fault. Frequently, fairy tale heroes do absolutely nothing at all to deserve whatever largess eventually befalls them. More than one leading character has reacted to adversity by sitting down and sobbing! But, as Vassilissa's little doll told her, "Never fear! Have a little to eat, and go to bed. The morning is wiser than the evening." Help always comes to the ones who are honest, hard-working, or dumb! The "fool of the world" somehow manages to befriend just the right combination of talented fellows, which proceeds to help him in his quest for the Tsar's daughter.

It would be impossible to avoid the issue of "wicked stepmothers" in this book, but it would be equally impossible to cover the subject extensively. Whole books (or long, erudite chapters in other books) have been written on the psychological implications of this character. Long treatises have been expounded on the place of this character in the repertoire of contemporary storytellers, and more than a few literary fairy tales have been written in an attempt to correct the imbalance in the portrayal of stepparents as evil. Although Freudian analysts have likened the bad stepmother to that mother who, for whatever reason, is unable or unwilling to fulfill a child's every wish immediately, this explanation does little to allay the genuine and understandable fears of stepmothers and their children. The suggestion has been made that these stories have no place in modern life, and certainly there are plenty of other stories to go around. A storyteller can easily eliminate those stories that mention stepparents from his or her programs.

There is, however, another way to deal with the problem of what to do with a story you love that contains a reference you don't: prepare. You can prepare yourself and your audience for the story by saying, "You know that there are a lot of things in stories that aren't real today, like ogres or monsters. Well, this next story has an evil stepmother. Now you know, and I know, that this is a story, and that is a story-kind of evil stepmother, and that's not the way it is in real life." In her cogent and down-to-earth book *The Ordinary and the Fabulous*, (Cambridge Univ. Pr., 1978) Elizabeth Cook writes, "Children are frightened of giants or dogs with eyes like mill-wheels as long as they feel that what happens in a story might literally happen to them. J. R. R. Tolkein has interpreted 'Is it true?' quite rightly. 'They mean: "I like this, but is it contemporary? Am I safe in my bed?" The answer "There is certainly no dragon in England today," is all that they want to hear'" (40).

If, however, these words (or some very like them) do not come trippingly off the tongue, or if you are in any doubt about the ability of your audience to distinguish between reality and fairy tale, then the only proper response is not to tell the story. Just as with those stories which promulgate a view of women that you find distasteful, it is better to refrain from telling them than to bastardize them in an attempt (doomed to failure!) to be politically or socially "correct."

The class of heroes/heroines is balanced by villains on one side, and by magical helpers on the other. Together they form the triumvirate of fairy tale classic characters. These three categories balance each other, and create endless plot possibilities as they are juggled with other classic elements to form fairy tales.

The enduring presence of stereotypical characters—"The Hero," "The Witch," "The Evil Stepmother"—has been both the blessing and the bane of many storytellers and parents' existences. They are staples of folk literature because they are so powerful and so clear. Since they are at best one- or two-dimensional, they are guideposts for the action and repositories for our expectations. [Evil is vanquished, the helpless and defenseless are triumphant; because this is possible, then it stands to reason that it is possible for a child (helpless) to survive against seemingly impossible odds (poverty, injustice) and overpowering forces (adults).] While it is not always possible for an adult to feel comfortable with every fairy-tale message—and there are some stories that harken back to centuries of racism and misogyny that are best left behind—we should try to see beyond our own fears of those traditional, stereotyped characters. Children who are old enough to enjoy fairy tales are already aware of the difference between reality and fantasy. And they are also aware of the ways in which stories *mimic* certain aspects of reality. Certain adults and children are, indeed, bullies. That doesn't mean children think that fairy tale ogres are wandering the playground! Of course, it's important to be sensitive to children's fears, but we should allow for the possibility that kids are more resilient than we give them credit for being.

CHAPTER 5

When Is a Stick Not a Stick?

Talisman: A wonder-working object; a charm possessing and transmitting certain qualities. . . . Many of the magic objects of folktale—the cap of invisibility, the seven-league boots, the self-setting table, etc.—can be classed as talismans (sic), for they have a positive power of themselves.

from *Funk & Wagnalls Standard Dictionary of Folklore, Mythology, and Legend.* Harper & Row, 1984.

When is a stick not a stick? When it's a magic wand, of course. In fairy tales, it's a sure bet that certain objects will take on unusual importance, as they can give the protagonist a magical leg-up in dealing with perilous situations. The use of these objects varies, according to the nature of the character who wields them, but they are usually given to our hero or heroine in recognition of acts of kindness, or to assist the character in pursuing his or her rightful path. This motif is so widely accepted that modern story-writers use it with facility. In "Petronella," by Jay Williams (from *The Practical Princess, and Other Liberating Fairy Tales,* Parents Magazine Press, 1978), the heroine is kind to an old man who, in gratitude, tells her what she must obtain in order to escape from the enchanter. Petronella works for the enchanter, and in payment for her service she requests and receives a comb, a mirror, and a ring. When, at the end of the story, she is being pursued, she throws the comb behind her, and it becomes a forest of trees. The mirror becomes a huge lake, and the ring becomes a snare to trap the enchanter. These images are almost identical to those in the Russian fairy tale about Vassilisa the Brave. (The difference is that Vassilisa escapes from the witch, Baba Yaga, but Petronella discovers that her pursuer is quite enamored of her—and he's no slouch himself—so she frees him! These are the kinds of plot twists that only modern literary stories can take.)

It's important for the teller to recognize that the magical powers of these objects is selective. I mean that the comb is just a comb until it is used in a particular way. As Freud is said to have remarked, "Sometimes a cigar is just a cigar."

Particular importance is given to those objects which are relics or remembrances: Vassilissa carries the doll her mother gave her before dying. The doll becomes not merely a reminder of, but also a spiritual link with the mother, who provides counsel to her daughter. Cinderella plants a hazel twig on her mother's grave, and the tree that grows from that twig becomes her guardian and comfort in her trials. Not only that, but "a little white bird always came to perch in the tree, and if Cinderella wished a wish, whatever it was, the bird would bring it to her." The twig truly is the original magic wand: a living thing that is a connection between the two worlds, a link to the dead, and to supernatural powers. The bird is the traditional spirit messenger of folk and fairy tales.

The properties of a "magic object" will always be appropriate to the element or the nature of the object. That is, an organic object has the power to grow, but an inorganic object will not. A boot might be capable of striding seven leagues, but it will not produce food. There is a kind of common sense relationship between the realistic properties of an object and the special powers it assumes in fairy tales. When you see a story that violates those rules, you have found either a rewritten story, one that has been clumsily doctored, or else a true iconoclast, the rare tale that follows a totally different internal logic that is specific to its own cultural messages.

When magic occurs in a fairy tale, it is of interest for several reasons: First, because it provides the hero (or, sometimes, the villain) with extra powers with which to accomplish his goal. That is, the magic object is an extension of the user, and can only perform in a way that is consistent with the user's will or ambitions. If the heroine is required by her tormentor to complete a task, the magic object will not destroy the villain. It can only help to perform the task. Secondly, the magic object will usually be something quite commonplace, something with which the listener is familiar. This fact serves to make the magical nature of the object even more remarkable! Think, for example, of the horror stories of such masters as Stephen King. If the scene is a spooky basement, then the events are too predictable. But if the horror occurs in a brightly sunlit park, then the impact is intensified. The same thing is true for magic. The most ordinary object creates a more extraordinary effect when it is found to possess magic powers.

Another noteworthy point about magic is that it never extends beyond what is needed. There is no waste, no excess when it comes to supernatural occurrences. If the spindle, shuttle, and needle (from the Grimms' story of the same name) wish to direct the Prince's attention to the young maid, they do not build a palace for her to inhabit. Instead, they decorate her humble hut with remarkable tapestries. In this way, the ordinary becomes exceptional.

The theme of transformation is so pervasive in fairy tales that it can be used as one of the markers for the classic European fairy tale genre. Objects, animals, people all change in the blink of an eye. They are changed in response to curses or blessings, because of the violation of taboos (eating or drinking forbidden foods, reading forbidden books, entering a forbidden room, etc.), or because of the possession of magic objects, ie., enablers. If I have a cloak of invisibility, then I can alter my appearance. Even ordinary, non-magic disguises, such as a cloak of moss (as in the British version of the story "Tattercoats") or a veil can constitute a transformation. "These disguises, whether of rags, animal skins, rushes or whatever, are, like the veil, a symbol of separation—both a physical separation from her true station in life and a spiritual severance of Paradise. . . . This removal of the disguise or veil is also a transformation symbol; . . ." (Cooper, 84). Myths also contain transformation motifs, but those motifs are frequently the point of a myth, whereas they are merely the path of the fairy tale. By this I mean that when the story tells how seven brothers danced up into the sky until they were changed into stars, the transformation is the end of the myth. But in a typical fairy tale setting, the brothers would have to perform some task as stars, or they might travel to another location, where they would then resume their proper form. In other words the transformation is a means to a larger end!

Some of these changes happen before the story starts—"off stage," if you will. They prepare the way for the action of the story. The mouse who shows up in response to the need for a "sweetheart" has already undergone one transformation, and is awaiting another. But even in this instance the fairy tale has no "history." In screen writing, people talk about the "back story," the history of the characters before the first frame of the movie. But fairy tales have no such pre-life. The transformations that are in place before the story starts are merely there to facilitate the story. The hero has no life outside of the fairy tale.

Transformation can be seen as either a boon or a curse, depending on the situation. The princess who has been changed into a frog will be able to find the suitor who sees past the exterior. So her transformation has actually been a blessing in disguise. On the other hand, the old man who is given three wishes soon realizes the dangers of this gift when he accidentally utters the fateful words, "I wish this pudding was on your nose!" But in all fairy tales, transformation is a means of ascending (if you are one of the "good" characters) or descending (if you are a "bad" character). The heroine will continue to change until she arrives at maturity, wholeness, what psychologists call "individuation"—the ability to recognize one's self as being separate and distinct from one's parents. A grown-up!

The ways in which the hero or heroine of a story utilizes a magic object can reflect growth, maturity, and a highly evolved ability to make choices and decisions. That's a fancy way of saying that the character changes in many of the same ways that children change. And the magic object which, at the beginning of the story is used selfishly, may later be used in a more considerate or generous fashion. If both the hero and the villain have the opportunity to use a magic object, they will each use it according to their natures.

In some stories the "object" is a creature, an animal which performs extraordinary acts to aid the protagonist. In the many classic fairy-tale motifs, *Grateful animals*, there are a variety of traditional scenarios: the protagonist either saves the life of a creature who is threatened, or refuses to perform some act of cruelty (unlike other story-characters). When this happens the animal may respond by giving the protagonist a talisman with which to summon magical powers. The fish who is rescued may give one of its own scales, the fox three hairs from his tail. If no object is given, then the animal simply says, "I will repay your kindness," or "Call on me if ever you are in need." And in this way a simple act of kindness takes on larger significance. If there is anything to be learned from this motif, it is that there is magic in each person when they choose to act with humanity and generosity of spirit. And it takes no special talent to practice "random, senseless acts of charity."

It would be a mistake to imagine that every magical event or object in a fairy tale can be explained. There is in every story at least a kernel of the inexplicable, the wondrous. And for generations children and adults have returned to fairy tales to savor the possibilities!

CHAPTER 6

Politics and Sex

> To talk about fairy tales today, especially feminist fairy tales, one
> must, in my opinion, talk about power, violence, alienation, social
> conditions, child-rearing and sex roles. It is no longer possible to
> ignore the connection between the aesthetic components of the
> fairy tales, whether they be old or new, and their historical function
> within a socialization process which forms taste, mores, values,
> and habits.
>
> from *Don't Bet on the Prince: Contemporary Feminist Fairy Tales in
> North America and England* by Jack Zipes. Routledge, 1989.

If you approach traditional, orally-transmitted fairy tales with a late-twentieth century set of sensibilities, you are bound to be disappointed. In many of the areas in which we have tried to change as individuals and as a society, fairy tales are hopelessly "politically incorrect." They are primarily the products of traditional, male-oriented, highly class-structured European cultures, and as such they are reflections of the ways in which power can be used, misused, circumvented, or ameliorated. Even non-European fairy tales tend to speak from a social and political and sexual context that some modern tellers find uncomfortable, to say the least. But if we only see the stories as being out of step with current thinking, then we miss the point. If we try to make the stories dance to the fashion of our time, then we run the risk of destroying all of the imaginative "what-if-ing," all of the theorizing, psychic healing, fun, and vicarious experimentation that these stories can provide. And yet, "The relationship between man and woman is one of the fundamentals of the fairy tales" (Cooper, 79).

One of the most frequent criticisms from modern storytellers concerns the treatment of women. The political reality of the Middle Ages is that women of high birth were valuable commodities. They were the legal possessions of their fathers, who could then bestow them upon a mate. High-born women were expected to be skilled in a variety of crafts—needlepoint, music, dance (as of the late Middle Ages, before which it was considered sinful), and housekeeping. This last including budgeting, for a woman would be expected to run the house when her husband was away fighting, hunting, or visiting other nobles. And, as is true even today, women had primary responsibility for child care. Girls were cared for exclusively by women until marriage, and boys until puberty, when the task of training them in "manly arts" was turned over to various instructors.

In houses of less than noble stature, a woman's position was somewhat different, although still inferior to a man's. The birth of a daughter could foretell real hardship, for while a son was responsible for maintaining his parents, a daughter would be married off, eventually to help care for someone else's parents. And a girl would have to have a dowery in order to find a good husband. As with her royal counterpart, a peasant girl had to learn certain skills: making cloth (spinning and weaving), churning butter, cooking and baking, basic healing skills, tending to animals. She, too, was the legal possession of her father (or, in his absence, the oldest male relative), but marriage was more likely to be negotiated with the consent of the woman, because there was less to be gained by forcing a woman to marry against her inclination. Expectations were different.

What is also true of both high- and low-born women is that, like their counterparts in every age, many found various paths, subtle or overt, to power. Since they were responsible for child rearing, women could and, one guesses, frequently did affect the messages that society gave about the value of girls. In European cultures, storytelling seems to have been an "equal opportunity employer." And, although there are notable examples of cultures in which formal storytelling was reserved for men, there are just as many instances of female bards, minstrels, and honored professional tellers. This does not even take into account the informal, hearthside storytelling that was probably a staple of medieval life. In *The World of Storytelling* storyteller, linguist, and collector Anne Pellowski cites instances of women as storytellers in France, Japan, Hungary, Russia, and India, as well as throughout the Latin countries.

Lüthi notes that ". . . the Grimm brothers' informants were predominantly women. And today children learn fairy tales mainly from their mothers, grandmothers, aunts, and female kindergarten and school teachers. . . . Furthermore, our era, whose character, despite everything, is still determined by men, feels the strong and clear need for a complementary antipole. The woman is assigned a privileged position, not only by social custom; in art and literature, as well, she has occupied a central position since the time . . . of the late Middle Ages" (*Once Upon a Time*, 136). Lüthi claims that this "privileged position" of women as symbols in art, as well as in the role of storytellers, explains the predominance of female characters in the stories. However, despite this fact, prior to the twentieth century, women only rarely shaped their own destinies, except in the stories.

Fairy-tale heroines frequently behave in atypical or socially unacceptable fashions: they leave home (and the protection of their fathers) to go out on quests—usually for a mate. Or they control their fates through the device of a riddle. In *The Merchant of Venice*, Portia's father has devised a test for all of her suitors, and she herself is grateful to him, and administers the test even after his death. Shakespeare may have borrowed this device from a popular folktale. The test involves guessing which of three caskets holds the princess' portrait. Since the caskets are of gold, silver, and lead, the choice tests the values of the suitors. Does this man equate marriage to the princess as a pure business venture, involving only material wealth? The theme of the princess who riddles with her suitors is echoed in the opera *Turandot*. In many fairy tales it is the princess herself who poses questions, riddles, or tests to suitors. By doing so she is able to control her own fate, and the man who succeeds is often not a prince, but a low-born man who is inventive, clever, persistent, patient, or possessed of simple common sense! Even a princess who is adverse to marriage finds herself won over by such qualities. They can then form a bond that will be stronger than conventional marriage. Freudian psychologists have theorized that the fairy-tale marriage of man and woman in a union that is born of equality and strength, not of compulsion, symbolizes the maturation of the individual, and the union of male and female aspects. "This search for the true partner occurs in all myth and religious allegory; it is the quest for personal completion in relationship and sharing, a resolution of contraries into unity, symbolized by the yin-yang opposites contained in the unifying circle" (Cooper, 79). The implication is that fairy tales are not depicting "real" men and women, but rather female and male aspects of a single individual. Unfortunately that analysis, while very appealing in the abstract, is basically unsatisfying for the storyteller. What is, perhaps, more useful to us is a sense of rightness, of appropriateness, that the story has, at its end, brought together the two who are worthy of each other. Any analysis that overemphasizes philosophy and sophistry denies the experience of the first teller! After all, the old woman who told the stories to the people gathered in front of the fire at the end of an exhausting day was not concerned with the yin-yang of a successfully integrated personality! She was reflecting her own past and present, through the prism of her own imagination. And so does every storyteller to this very day.

The greatest influence that has been brought to bear on European fairy tales, the ones we naively call "the classic fairy tales," was that very imaginative element, the influence of the teller. The grandmothers, the spinsters (again, notice the use of the job title to designate a woman of a particular rank), the crones, the wise-women—these were the primary transmitters of fairy tales. Other stories—harvest-related tales, work and/or war stories—may have been told by men, but the stories that lingered were the stories that were mixed with the smell of smoke from the hearth and the sound of knitting or other women's crafts in the background! So why, you might ask, are so many of the stories antagonistic or downright cruel to women? In part because of the nature of the hierarchy in which they lived. A teller can only reflect what she knows or what she can hypothesize, imagine, or foresee! Also, it is fair to say that some small number of fairy tales have a cruelty that is not directed specifically at women. But the other side of the story is that women are as often depicted as possessing great powers, either through the choices they make or through the use of supernatural or spiritual forces. Women can affect events because of their appetites, sexual or other. In Rapunzel, the pregnant mother has an unnatural desire for rampion, or rapunzel—a kind of lettuce. The force of that desire drives her husband into the witch's garden, and precipitates the bargain that is the focus of the story.

In certain other stories the heroine is able to discover the hiding place of all potential suitors. All, that is, until our humble hero comes along. Her destiny (fate, strength) is to test, and his is to help and be helped. In the Grimms' tale, "The Little Sea Hare," the princess can look out of the twelve windows of her tower and see all things on the earth and the sea, and the air, so she can find the hiding places of all would-be suitors. When they fail to hide from her, she has them killed, and their heads mounted on pikes. When ninety-seven heads adorn the palace grounds she thinks, "Now I shall be free forever!" In that one phrase she (and, by extension, the woman who told the story) expresses a truth about marriage in her time. Marriage can be equivalent to bondage if it joins unequal parties. But the humble man who, through the assistance of the animals he has befriended, manages to hide from the princess successfully is a match for her in wit and in persistence. And she recognizes that. Even after his first two failed attempts, she doesn't order him executed. The reason for her decision to spare him is not in the text. Only the tellers, the truly expressive, suggestive, real and raunchy women who told the stories, could have given their audiences the reasons for the princess's restraint, because it is not in the written language of the story. It is understood and suggested, as so much story meaning is, in the glance of the teller. The princess makes choices that are confluent with her recognition of the true value of this man. By doing that, by making choices and by accepting the consequences of their actions, women exercise real power.

There is really only one important "rule" concerning the depiction of women (or, for that matter, other minorities) in fairy tales. It is this: If the story makes you even a little uncomfortable, don't tell it. There are thousands of fairy tales, hundreds of thousands of folktales, myths, legends, all waiting to be told. If your impulse is to "improve" the story, to alter it or fix it or adjust it, then my advice is leave it alone. It is not your story to tell. Find the story that speaks to you in its own voice, and tell that one. It is far better to lose a story that projects messages that are anathema to you than to castrate the story to serve your agenda. Just let it go.

CHAPTER 7

What's My Motivation?

The simpleton . . . illustrates the spontaneous acceptance of things as they are, complete naturalness in action without ulterior motives, as well as openness of mind in recognizing limitations and being ready to accept aid, be it natural or supernatural, when faced with difficulties outside ordinary experience.

from *Fairy Tales: Allegories of the Inner Life* by J. C. Cooper.
Aquarian Press, 1983.

In a standard show-business joke, a young actor asks the director, "What's my motivation?" "If you don't do it," says the director, "you're fired." In real life, people have motives. In fairy tales, although there may be reasons for certain actions, characters do what they must as a result of situation and because of their essential natures. In fact, plot is definitely very low on the list of fairy tale essentials. Characters are confronted with strangely arbitrary options, magical helpers appear at just the right moments, the third (or youngest) child will inevitably emerge victorious: very few fairy tales utilize original or "realistic" plot lines. Max Lüthi declares, "Motivations are not obligatory in the fairytale. They may be there: The hero's going out into the unknown is almost always justified. . . . Other things are not given any justification, not motivated, not explained" (*The Fairytale as Art Form and Portrait of Man*, Indiana University Press, 1984, 67).

In a random sampling of fairy tales you might find the following "motives" for action: The desire/yearning for a mate; the need to "learn fear"; idle curiosity; laziness; fear of death; quest for _____ (fill in the blank: honor, wealth, revenge, magic powers, food, the water of life, a feather from the Firebird, three hairs from the beard/head of the Devil, a "real" princess . . . etc.) All of these, though reasonable in a fairy-tale sort of way, are a far cry from the complexities of real life. "[But] the general human demand for motivation always competes with the genre, and it is the battle between the two that gives life to the fairytale. . . . the fairytale has motivated and unmotivated side by side" (Lüthi, 113).

In keeping with the hypothesis that people (and story characters) reveal themselves by their choices and actions, it would seem that the fairytale plots exists primarily to allow the characters the opportunity to grow in response to trials and challenges, and to examine their true natures. The oldest child may seek to save the princess out of a sense of bravado; the second child tries because of "me-too-ism"; but the third child goes out of a sense of destiny. It is his fate, because of his birth position, to venture and to succeed. Each character has the chance, within the action of the story, to display his or her best and worst natures. Even "our hero" may take a wrong step, make a selfish or ill-informed choice, ignore good advice (usually several times before the lesson is learned!). But those choices are like a child's mistakes: they are the vehicles for growth.

The story forces the protagonist to confront his fears and longings, because only by doing so, by running a physical and emotional gauntlet, can he ascend to a higher plane of existence. It is not by accident that many protagonists (would-be heroes or heroines) are forced at some point in the tale to choose whether or not to forfeit that possession which is most dear to them. The Miller's Daughter can only become Queen by nearly losing her child. There is an understanding, in fairy tales, that wisdom comes at a price. If the oldest daughter requests a dress of gold, and the second of silver, then the youngest daughter will inevitably request some garment far more humble. At first glance that might seem to be a "good" choice, but in the code of fairy tales she has shamed and embarrassed her sisters by blatantly pointing out their weaknesses, and she will have to pay dearly for her too obvious humility. Real hardship will be endured (banishment) before the heroine can evolve to her proper place as consort to a more powerful and wealthy man. In this resolution, the fairy tale is a reflection of its own time and sensibilities. There can be no more prestigious position in the hierarchy of a monarchical society than royalty. One can get there by accident of birth, or by marriage or adoption (only in fairy tales can one achieve royalty by cooking a broth for the prince or by answering three riddles!). In the modern equivalent the story might come out of the notion that "anyone can grow up to become president."

But we are not talking about real wealth or power here or at least not exclusively. The great and abiding strength of fairy tales is that they mirror our own growth, rites of passage, losses, gains, and eventual ascension to adulthood. "The tension of fairy tales," writes Lüthi, "their inner dynamism, depends very little on the question What's going to happen?—for the outcome is more or less clear to the accustomed fairytale listener, especially because the happy ending for the hero or heroine, with whom the male and female listeners respectively can identify, is as good as certain. That the same listener wishes to hear the same fairytale several times—completely in contrast to the case, say, of the joke—shows that it sets in motion a pattern of internal experience, sets off a sequence of tension and relief of tension, of concentration and relaxation, similar in effect to that of a musical work, whose interest is also not exhausted by a single hearing and which one needs to hear time and again, since the effect is deepened through repeated listening" (Lüthi, 73). Fairy tales place our inner struggles right up there with the conflict to be worthy of and to inherit a throne. Our hopes and aspirations and dreams take on a grander metaphor. That is not merely psychobabble, as you can see if you ask a child about his or her favorite story. A child can talk about battling injustice, about being generous and gracious, about fighting dragons (adults) and ogres (schoolyard bullies) because of the context of story. In fact, as more and more educators are discovering, children who have a rich fairy tale repertoire are able to see the possible consequences of their actions, even to solve problems and conflicts in a greater variety of ways, not all of which are violent. The violence in the stories (sword-play, etc.) is translated into a more appropriate set of actions: standing up to a bully, or defending a weaker child. In fact, a preponderance of stories offers a variety of non-violent techniques for solving problems: negotiation, co-operation, or the out-maneuvering of an evil opponent. There is instinctive nobility in children that is reinforced by fairy tales, and that nobility can remain latent in children who have never become comfortable with the world of story. Fairy tales provide us with the safe opportunity to play out our worst fears and our dearest hopes, and perhaps, come to an understanding that reality lies somewhere in between the two.

CHAPTER 8

How to Start: The Tools of the Trade

The discriminating features of storytelling have to do with the relationship between the story, the teller, and the audience during the telling. . . . Regardless of the means by which a storyteller becomes one or learns the art, the storyteller is, in many respects, the tool and servant of the culture and the property of the literature.

Overall, a story is a story because it employs a recognizable set of general conventions or features that give it its identity as 'story.' However, each story is a different arrangement of the elements of story structure. . . . A specific story is recognizable and distinct, because it embeds story content and manipulates story rules in keeping with its own special formula. The teller must recognize both the generalizable aspects of a given story structure and the special structural effects that make a story unique.

from *Storytelling Process and Practise* by Norma J. Livo and Sandra A. Rietz. Libraries Unlimited, 1986.

Why Bother?

There are more than a few storytellers or would-be storytellers who might say that there is no point concerning oneself with the meaning(s) of fairy tales. After all, they argue, the original tellers didn't get all worked up over the social/political/gender implications of the stories, so why should we? And, you could add, they are just stories. I mean, kids will listen and enjoy, so why bother worrying about the meaning of this word or that phrase, or the significance of this color or that number?

Well, there are at least two reasons for all this research and investigation. First, because we do not live in the world of the original tellers. This means that implications which were fairly obvious to both the tellers and the listeners are now fairly obscure. Any child who lived in the fifteenth century would have understood what it meant to be a miller (the position of that man in society, the ease or difficulty of his work, the contacts and dependencies he would have established). But to a modern listener—even an adult—none of those vital pieces of information are readily available. We must make a conscious effort, at least the first time we tell or listen to the story, to make the necessary connections. Without those vital indicators we lose at least part of the meaning of the story.

The second reason is more esoteric, and it applies mostly to those who wish to tell stories with a high "comfort margin" (that is, with ease and familiarity). So this reason is applicable to anyone who uses or hopes to use storytelling in his or her professional life. We study and concern ourselves with meanings so that we always have at least 10 percent more story than we tell! Think of an athlete who is preparing to run a race. He never knows which of the other runners might prove to be a threat, who might come from behind, or who might have a "kick" at the end. So the runner practices full out; he gives 100 percent in practice, with the hope that if he runs at an optimal 85 percent, he will still have some strength in reserve. Then his running seems fluent and coordinated, not desperate! The same thing is true of a performer. If you understand only the surface meaning of the story, then your storytelling will be limited to the words. It won't have the kind of resonance that comes from knowledge held in reserve. The difference is obvious to even the most casual listener. One storyteller seems to have given up their entire understanding of the story with the words; they are "used up." Another storyteller tells the same story, perhaps with virtually the same words, but they seem to have more to give. Their words contain subtleties of intonation that inform the listener in ways that a simple recitation of the words cannot.

I can give you an example of what I mean: I was in a bookstore where a storyteller was entertaining a group of children with an Efik-Ibibio

(Nigerian) folktale, "Why Sun, Moon, and Stars Live in the Sky." It's a story that I tell, so I stopped to listen. When she got to the place in the story where the Ocean says, "But my children are still outside. Shall I bring them in?" and the Sun says, "Yes, of course," (even though his house is going to be flooded), the storyteller said, "Now, wasn't that a foolish thing to say? Wasn't Sun stupid to invite the Ocean's children to come in?" At that moment I knew that the teller knew nothing about the story except the words! Because, in the Efik-Ibibio tradition it is an obligation—no, an honor—to extend an offer of hospitality to all the relatives of a guest. Having invited the Ocean in the first place, Sun could not possibly refuse to entertain all the children, aunts, uncles, and cousins of the Ocean! The storyteller took that simple tenet of life, and called it stupid. I'm sure she didn't mean to be insulting, but that's how it turned out. Perhaps it is unreasonable to expect that the storyteller might have known that, but for that very reason—because we can never be completely certain of the mores and standards of another society—it is doubly important that the storyteller use value-judgment words like "stupid" with care.

We study the meanings as a way of showing respect for the stories, for their progenitors, and for our listeners.

In Your Toolbox

In order to "get a handle" on a story, you may have to become a combination treasure hunter, researcher, historian, linguist, anthropologist, and theologian! Not all of these contexts are required for each story, but the point is that you'll need to sharpen your investigative skills. And there are more ways of analyzing or focusing on stories than could possibly be included in this volume. But here are some ideas to begin your exploration.

STITH AND MARGIE

That's Stith Thompson, the creator (with Finnish folklorist Antti Aarne) of *The Types of the Folktale: A Classification and Bibliography* (Suomalainen Tiedeakatemia, 1973), and Margaret Read MacDonald, the creator of *The Storyteller's Sourcebook: A Subject, Title and Motif Index to Folklore Collections for Children* (Gale Research/Neal-Schuman, 1982). Aarne published his basic work on folktale type classification in 1910. Thompson extended Aarne's research in 1928 and again in 1961. He also created the *Motif-Index of Folk-Literature* in 1932 (updated and presented in a six-volume set, published by the University of Indiana Press, between 1955 and 1958). One type number is assigned to each tale type within such large, general classifications, as Animal Tales (Types 1–299), Magic Tales (Types 300–800), Religious Tales, Romantic Tales, etc. A tale type might be *Transformation: Animal to Person* or *Helpful Animal*. Motifs are small divisions within particular tale types.

MacDonald's *Storyteller's Sourcebook* is organized in several ways: you can find stories by motif number, by popular title, or by subject. This volume deals only with children's literature, and only with material readily available in English. Most stories have several motifs, and *The Storyteller's Sourcebook* allows you to find a story title and then locate variants or other stories with the same or similar motifs.

Another excellent resource tool is *A Guide to Folktales in the English Language*, by D. L. Ashliman (Greenwood Press, 1987). Like MacDonald, Ashliman surveys many collections of folktales, but he lists stories in tale-type order. So, for example, Type 160 is in the general group called Animal Tales, and this one is *Grateful Animals: Ungrateful Man*. One of the motifs found in that section is B511 *Maid promises to wed horse*. (Yes, there actually is such a division!) Ashliman's book deals only with material that was created, collected, or compiled for adult use, but this includes a number of what might be considered "crossover" books.

For examples of how one might analyze folktales, one of the best sources is *World Folktales: A Scribner Resource Collection*, by Atelia Clarkson and Gilbert T. Cross (Charles Scribners Sons, 1980). In addition to presenting a variety of ways of using folktales in the classroom (elementary, secondary, and college), this book follows each story with a detailed type and motif analysis, and a list of variants. So, for example, "The Travels of a Fox" is identified as Tale Type 1655 *The Profitable Exchange* and Type 170 *The Fox Eats His Fellow Lodger*. The principle motifs are listed as C322 *Tabu: looking into a bag*; K251.1 *The eaten grain and the cock as damages*;

K526 *Captor's bag filled with animals or objects while captive escapes*; K525.6 *Escape leaving dog as substitute*; and Z47 *Series of trick exchanges*. As you can see, some of these overlap. This analysis is followed by a list of five variants, and information to help you locate them.

One way to understand the matter of tale types and motifs is to imagine an umbrella that can encompass many stories with the same basic premise:

> A widower with one child marries a widow who has children of her own. When the father dies, the woman is cruel to his child and favors her own children. Eventually, the orphaned child achieves success, marries royally, and the other siblings are punished.

The story? Cinderella, of course. In fact, the Cinderella story is so easily identifiable that it is the title of its own tale type, 510A. Even in certain elements of the familiar story are changed—for example, if the siblings are all male instead of female—you can still identify the basic premise as Cinderella. This tale type is one of the most widespread in world literature. If you make allowances for cultural differences, you can find Cinderella stories in virtually every language and every culture. Some scholars estimate that there are more than three hundred distinct Cinderella variants extant. Even when certain very important plot elements change, the core of the story remains intact. For example, in one Ojibway story, a widower has three daughters, and the two oldest are abusive of their little sister. She, however, succeeds (through her honesty and essentially kind nature) in marrying the culture hero. So, even though there is no "evil stepmother" (the two older sisters fulfill the function of the antagonist in this story), the tale is still a Cinderella type.

Among the various Cinderella stories, there are important distinctions: differences of culture markers, gender, plot twists, even symbol and outcome. In the Grimms' story, "Aschenputtel," the youngest daughter plants a hazel twig (magic wand) over her mother's grave. This grows into a tree, which is watered by her tears and listens to her sorrows. In some stories, the older siblings are repentant and are consequently forgiven. In other variants, they are transformed, as punishment. In the Ojibway tale, the two sisters are changed into aspen trees, who still quake and tremble at the approach of their brother-in-law, Strong Wind. This motif, in turn, transforms the story into a blend of fairy tale and origin legend, as it explains the beginnings of the quaking aspens, and the reasons for their violent trembling. In the classic German version, the sisters have their eyes pecked out by pigeons, and so "for their wickedness and falseness they were punished with blindness for the rest of their lives." In the Perrault story, "Cinderella," which is heavily "literature-ized," the sisters are forgiven, and taken into the palace. These different plot turns and subplots can be boiled down to one sentence each, and so, they constitute "motifs" within the story. For example, *Why aspen trees tremble* is Motif A2762.1. The motif of the *Abused youngest daughter* is L52. *Lowly heroine marries prince*, Motif L162, can also be found in many stories that are not Cinderella-types.

So, if you look at the "umbrella" of Cinderella-type stories, you'll see myriad different tales which share certain primary features and can all be identified as the same type. But the differences in plot structure, characters, objects that act (like slippers, hazel wands, and such) can be defined as motifs, with many of them occurring in each story. The type is the largest defining factor, the umbrella that encompasses many stories. The motifs are the moments, the elements that distinguish between variants.

This is the kind of research that expands your understanding of the story by giving you access to different world views of fairy tale patterns. Just as is true of the hundreds of Cinderella-type stories from different cultures, it can only enhance our appreciation for all the stories we choose to tell if we read as many as possible of the other versions.

There are dozens of other reference tools: annotated bibliographies, lists, collections. Those can be fairly expensive, and you needn't buy most of them. That's what libraries are for! (See Appendix A for a list of reference tools that are probably available from your public library.)

This may seem like a lot of trouble and work for a fairy tale, but there are good reasons for putting out the effort. If you invest time and energy in the research, the story will become part of you. You will own it, so to speak. And the way to start believing that you can actually get inside fairy tales is to recognize that stories fall into types, within the types there are distinct motifs. When you can feel knowledgeable about the story structure, you can tell it with greater confidence.

DIALOGUE WITH A CHARACTER

Write down the questions that occur to you. By writing them down, you force yourself to formulate the questions in a careful, cogent fashion. You can ask a character why she makes certain choices, and then speculate on the answers. Write those down, too. This method is obviously not appropriate with every story, and you have to remember that these are not "real" people with realistic motives or reactions. So a question like, "Why did you choose the middle road?" will not have an answer that concerns road conditions! Perhaps a good answer for an adventurous character might be, "It was the path that looked inviting." For a more timid type it might be, "The other roads looked less traveled, more dangerous" or "I just did 'Eeny meenie miny moe' and chose one!"

MAKE LISTS

Sometimes the way to "get into" a story is by listing various elements: Where does the story take place? (Outdoors, indoors, hut, castle, mountain cave, etc.) If the word choice seems particular, how often does the story use a specific description or adjective? How many male and female characters? In some stories even the moon or a tree is given a gender. List anything that seems fascinating to you.

CHART OR MAP

If the path of the story is elusive—or even if it's not—try drawing a scene-by-scene road map of the story. Be creative! You can make it like a comic strip, or a landscape drawing, or a machine diagram. Whatever seems the best technique to give you a visual sense of the story.

PHYSICAL GESTURES/FACIAL GESTURES

If there were a list of the most popular questions that are asked by beginning storytellers, the one after "How do you memorize all those words?" would be "What do you do with your hands?" It is a dead giveaway of a beginner that she or he insists on choreographing hand and face movements, as if movement, in and of itself, somehow enhances the telling. While it is true that experienced tellers sometimes seem to have beautiful or evocative movements, the correct "path" is for the interior of the story to dictate the moves, not for the moves to be laid on top like a costume. A better way to think about gesture is to imagine it as the result of an idea or emotion, not the indicator!

Try practicing the story with your hands in your pockets! If you come to a moment when it feels almost painful not to gesture, then that is an appropriate, meaning-driven motion. If the gesture is "designed" by the teller, it is usually false. When it is impulse driven, it cannot go wrong. Like every "rule," this one has exceptions: I have, on occasion, added American Sign Language to some of my stories. That is certainly a case of gesture by design. But my criteria for that choice are: If there is a deaf or hearing impaired audience, is this a story that I can communicate without breaking the flow? If there is no deaf or hearing impaired audience member, does this story have a particular style or timing or *something* that calls for the signs? If the answer to each question is "no," then I don't sign it.

The same rules of thumb hold true for facial gestures. If you were to look across a crowded room at a conversation that was taking place out of your range of hearing, you would be able to tell the difference between someone pretending to listen and someone who was really engaged, wouldn't you? Even if the smile looked real, the body posture would usually betray uneasiness. I recall an acting class where the coach was trying to get the student to "stop acting concerned. Just do what you have to do, and say the words, and if you are really invested in the moment, then your face will do the rest." That's true in life, and it's true in storytelling. It's fairly obvious, but for some reason the obvious tends to go right out the window when we are nervous. The key is to know the story so well that your entire focus is on the telling, not on your hands or your eyebrows or anything else. Later, after you can communicate the story with ease, you can monitor your posture, if you need to, but that is certainly not part of the preparation process.

Non-Western Stories

The definition of fairy tale breaks down somewhat when you look at stories from "native" or indigenous peoples. Typically, if a character changes shapes, or moves back and forth between the world of humans and that of animals, then that is a magical occurrence, and the narrative qualifies as a fairy tale. Not so among people who live in a direct relationship with the earth and the other creatures on it. Consequently, the standards which apply to stories from, say, the Iroquois or the Ghanain traditions are different from the ones that apply to more industrialized or urban cultures. These stories fall firmly into the category of folktale, and some may have elements of magic in them. For the sake of clarity, I have not tried to "parse" any of these stories, but I would like to take some time to discuss the nature of the differences, and perhaps that will suggest ways in which a storyteller might approach them with respect.

Whenever you tell a story, you have an obligation to the culture from which the story takes its life, but especially in the case of cultures and traditions that are not your own. Assumptions that one makes about story language simply may not hold water in these stories. When I first started telling stories, I was particularly captured by a folktale from *The King's Drum* by Harold Courlander (Harcourt, Brace, and World, 1962). The story "The Song of Gimmile," was about a minstrel who is "paid" for his stories and songs with a beating! In return, another man creates a song of ridicule about the king. When a Western audience thinks about ridicule they might remember the childhood rhyme, "Sticks and stones may break my bones, but names will never harm me." But in Mali, where this story originates, the idea of ridicule is serious. An African king can only govern with the respect of the people, and ridicule undermines his office. In this story and in this culture, ridicule is far more damaging than a beating! As I understood this concept, the telling of the story changed. The "telling" words are, "You did not have to beat me, but you did; now you cannot take it back. Gimmile did not have to write a song, but he did; now that song is a real thing. It cannot be taken away."

In that instance, the cultural marker was a matter of values. In some stories it is a matter of definition. The culture hero known as the Trickster exists in many stories from countries and traditions as diverse as Native American (Coyote, Raven, Jay), Haitian (Ti Malice), Norse (Loki), Dutch (Til Eulenspiegel), . . . the list goes on and on. But in each instance, the word "trickster" holds different connotations for each culture group. In some it implies clown or fool, and in others it means something far more serious and devious. Popular retellings frequently reduce the character to its lowest level, degrading those cultures that believe that the Trickster is a creative force. In various star-stories (which are not usually defined as fairy tales, but share some of the same traits), Coyote is frequently represented as having "decorated the night" by haphazardly hurling stars into the air. But without the proper respect for Coyote as a life force, he is reduced to the level of a cartoon character, a bumbler, instead of a divine clown, which is closer to the truth. In Barry Holstun Lopez's sometimes funny, frequently scatalogical, always insightful collection, *Giving Birth to Thunder, Sleeping with His Daughter: Coyote Builds North America* (Avon Bard, 1977), Coyote gets to express the full range of thought and action of which he is capable. It might be a great way to gain insight into this culture hero to read stories that one would never tell to children!

It may not be possible to do the kind of research on these stories that one might do on European fairy tales, but there are practical ways of getting into the heart of the tribal/native stories. First, be creative in searching out information. If you can't find story variants, then it is even more important to read other tales from the same culture. Whether you tell these others or not, they are your "background research," and can lead you to make certain choices in how you tell the story. Something that seems cute and comical at first reading can turn out to be macabre! Immerse yourself, even if only for a few days, in other stories. Other sources for information are obvious: your library's photo collection, anthropological essays, recordings of the native language. Museum displays may actually come to life if you run the story through your mind as you look at the clothes or implements. This is a cinematic technique that can add a truthful quality to your telling.

If all else fails, take the advice of Vi Hilbert, a Native Skagit elder and storyteller. At a conference in New York City, she was asked, "What if you really love a story, but it's not your own culture? Is it right to tell that story?" She replied that if one tells with humility, if you say, "I do not pretend to know everything about it, but here is a story that I love," then your storytelling must be right. It's only when you pretend to be an authority that the storytelling becomes an offense against the culture of its birth. And I would add, never stop searching!

I have told the stories in Part II for many years. I have tried to choose fairy tales from a wide variety of cultures. Each story will be presented in written form, but pretty much in the same words that I use to tell it. However, the written versions may not "look" the same as they sound. The actual telling of a story involves elements of timing, style, physicality—all of which transform the meaning. In cases where the printed version would be confusing, I have added or changed the wording to keep the story that you see on the page consistent with the story one would hear/see.

PART II

The Stories

CHAPTER 9

Varied Methods of Preparation

The whole point of this book is to change the way you tell fairy tales; to make them more exciting to prepare, and to use that preparation to give yourself a clearer picture of the story line. Whether you opt for diagrams or lists or thesaurus entries, it's useless if you can't (or don't) tell the story! Read the following sample stories. The "work" sections should give you ideas that you can apply to other stories. It doesn't matter whether you start in the beginning or the middle or the end of a story. Take your insights where you find them! Then take all your research and arrange it in the chronological order of the story.

Then try taking the drawings, lists, q's&a's—whatever, and telling the story while following your own research notes. It's as if you were reading the text, but in reality you are reading the subtext, the meanings behind the words. Try going back and forth from the words (text) to the subtext to see how they compare. You might find additional images that had not been obvious on first or even second reading.

I usually tell a new story to one other person, sometimes very early in my study. The exercise is just to get the words out of my mouth. I sometimes tell the story even if I don't know it very well! Then I go back to the text and do the kind of work that I describe in this section. Every time I learn something new about the story, I tell it again. My suggestion to would-be tellers is, "Cultivate good and patient friends!" Eventually the words of the story and the meanings/implications you've uncovered mesh to create a working version—your personal, tellable adaptation.

The Twelve Huntsmen (Brothers Grimm)

This was the first story that I consciously tried to analyze and diagram, so although this isn't a particularly well-known story, or one with a lot of familiar motifs, I'd like to start with it.

The story begins, in most translations, with the words, "There was once a prince who had a bride whom he loved very much." I tell it differently, for reasons that will be discussed after my adaptation of the story.

THE STORY:

There was once a prince who traveled through many different lands until he came to a kingdom where he met a princess. And they fell in love. Well, one day they were sitting together, happy with each other, when a messenger came from the prince's kingdom to say that the old king was dying, and he sent for his son to come quickly.

When the prince heard that he rose, and he took his bride's hands in his and he said, "I must leave you now. But I will return for you and you shall be my Queen." Then he took the ring from his finger and gave it to her. "Wear this for me—as a keepsake." Then he kissed her and he left.

When the prince arrived at his father's side he found that, indeed, the old king was dying, and he said to his son, "Promise me something. Promise me that when I die you will marry the girl I have chosen for you." And the boy was so upset, and so confused that he promised. Then the old king died. The old king was buried, the new king was crowned, and then the young man felt he had to keep his promise to his father. So he sent out messengers throughout the land to say that the new young king would marry thus-and-such a princess.

When the true bride heard that, she became sick. She could not eat, she couldn't sleep, she grew thin and pale. Her father was so worried, he said, "Dearest child, tell me what can I do for you? Anything, and if it can be done, then it will be done." And she thought for a moment and then she said, "Bring me eleven girls exactly like me in face and in form and in stature." And he said, "If it can be done, it will be done." So the king sent out his messengers, and sure enough, they found eleven girls just exactly like his daughter in face, and in form, and in stature. And the princess looked at them, and was pleased. So she called a tailor, and she had the tailor make her twelve costumes—huntsmen's costumes. The eleven girls put on eleven costumes, and she put on the twelfth. Then the twelve girls mounted horses, and they rode to the castle of the new, young king.

When they got there, they said would he not hire them to be his huntsmen? And the king looked at her, and he did not know her. So he said yes, since they were such pretty folk, he would hire them. So they became the king's twelve huntsmen. And every day he went out hunting with them, and every day they grew dearer and dearer to him. Especially the one who was their leader.

Now the king had an advisor who was a lion, and this lion was a most remarkable creature, for he could see all things that were hidden. One day the king and the lion were talking together, and the lion said, "You think you have twelve huntsmen there, don't you?" And the king said, "Yes! That's what I have. Twelve huntsmen." But the lion said, "You are wrong. You have twelve girls." The king said, "How could you prove such a thing?" And the lion said, "Test them! Take some peas, and strew them in the chamber. Then call your huntsmen to you. Now when men walk, they walk with a firm tread, and the peas will not move. But girls! The peas will go skipping and skittering all around." So the king ordered it done.

But the king had a servant who loved the twelve huntsmen, and he went to warn them. So when the princess was alone with her girls she said, "You must force yourselves! Walk like men, with a firm tread. Don't even look down."

And that's what they did. They walked straight through the chamber with a firm tread, and not a single pea moved! So the king said to the lion, "There, you see? You were mistaken." But the lion said, "No, they knew they were being tested. Test them again. Take twelve spinning wheels and put them in the chamber. Now men, they will pay no attention. But girls will go over and admire them, and see how well they are made." So the king thought it was a good idea, and he ordered it done.

But that servant went and warned them, so when the princess was alone with her girls she said to them, "You must force yourselves! Walk straight through the chamber. Look neither to the right nor to the left, and don't even glance at the spinning wheels." And they did. They walked straight through the chamber, they looked neither to the right nor to the left, and they didn't even glance at the spinning wheels. So the king said to the lion, "There! You see? You were wrong! They are men." The lion said, "No, test them again!" But by this time the king would not believe his advisor, and he had the lion thrown out of court.

Now, time went by, and time went by, and every day they went out hunting with the king, and every day they grew dearer and dearer to him. Especially the one who was their leader. Then one day a messenger came to say that the new bride was coming. When the true bride heard that, she felt her heart break inside of her, and she fell from her horse in a faint. The king hurried to help his dear huntsman, and when he lifted her up, the glove came off of her hand, and there he saw his own ring. Then he looked at her, and he knew her. And he said, "You are mine, and I am yours, and no power on earth can change that."

Then he sent a messenger to the new bride and told her to go home, because he already had a bride. And, after all, when one has found the old key, one doesn't need the new one! And as for the lion? Why he was brought back to the court. Hadn't he been telling the truth all along? (adaptation by the author)

THE WORK:

When I first "found" this story (or, more correctly, when it found me), I thought it was rather odd. The ending seemed abrupt, and it seemed strange to me that the prince should not know her. After dismissing the story two or three times, I began to feel that it was important to me on a subconscious level, so I researched several translations of the story. Slowly I learned it, and began to tell it in small, "safe" settings. Then, in a class that I was teaching, I talked about diagraming stories, and about lists, and a student asked me to give an example. Since I had just told this story, I began to play with the ideas we were discussing, and the following lists and charts came about as a result of that class discussion and of subsequent work.

WORDS

First I made a list of all the words or phrases that were, to my mind, interesting.

Bride—"He took his *bride*'s hands in his . . ."
Keepsake—"Wear this for me, as a *keepsake*."
Face, form, stature—"Find me eleven girls exactly like me *in face, and in form, and in stature*."
Know—"He looked at her and he did not *know* her."
The lion.
The twelve spinning wheels.
The servant—"who loved the twelve huntsmen"
"When one has found the old key, one doesn't need the new one."

First, I began by looking at different translations of the same story. In some, the words which I found interesting were different. So in several translations the word "know" was rendered "recognize." The word "bride" was used pretty consistently, as were "face, form, and stature" (or "face, figure and stature"). The servant was, in some versions, "fond" of the huntsmen or "had their best interests in mind." The lion was always a lion, and everything else was pretty consistent from version to version.

Then, without any preconceptions about the implications of those words, I started drawing a kind of diagram of the plot of the story, using the symbols from Claude Levi-Strauss' analyses of myths. And I added a few twists of my own (see diagrams, p. 54–55).

Then I went to the thesaurus and dictionary to look at the words "bride" and "know."

Bride—All I could come up with was the standard meaning, "new-lywed" until I went to the *Oxford English Dictionary*. There I found out that in the time from the eleventh through the sixteenth centuries the word "bride" referred to any woman who was betrothed, or promised in marriage. She would be a bride from the time of the declaration of an intention to marry until the actual wedding. Later, the woman was called a bride after the posting of the bans in church. After the marriage she would be a wife. So to say that the prince had a bride means that he had given his promise. He had declared his intention to marry the princess.

Know—Here I had better luck with the thesaurus. Under "know" you find "be apprised, be certain, be friends, experience, have knowledge, recognize and understand." I checked out "recognize" first, since I had run into that other translation. "Recognize" gives us "know, tell, distin-

THE TWELVE HUNTSMEN
Diag. I

$\triangle$ = male $\bigcirc$ = female   K = king
P = prince or
princess

Betrothed (Promised)

Diag. II

Old king dies . . . new king is crowned.

Diag. III

Princess and all 11 women
disguise themselves as men.

Diag. IV

The lion can see

Question:
Can the servant see?
Is the servant male or female?

guish, make out, identify, and realize," among others. I became intrigued with "realize." "The prince looked at her, and he did not realize her." Then I checked "understand" and I got "comprehend, conceive, appreciate, fathom, grasp," and more. As you can see, there is more to "know" than one might think. From "have knowledge" comes "perceive, be cognizant of, be conscious, possess." And from the Bible comes "to have conjugal knowledge of." So, when I put all the inferences together I decided that the prince did not, indeed, know the princess. He didn't recognize her, because of the disguise, he hadn't had sex with her, because

Diag. V

Test 1 = Peas
Test 2 = (Swords) vs. Spinning Wheels

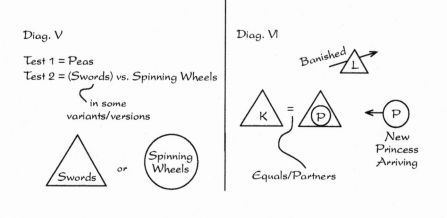

in some
variants/versions

Swords   or   Spinning Wheels

Diag. VI

Banished

K = (P)   ← P

Equals/Partners

New Princess Arriving

Diag. VII

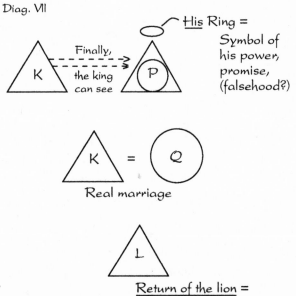

Finally, the king can see

K ---→ (P)

<u>His</u> Ring =
Symbol of his power, promise, (falsehood?)

K = Q

Real marriage

L

<u>Return of the lion</u> =
Animal? Sex? Instinct?

she was his bride, his intended, and not his wife, and he really didn't understand what she was capable of.

Perhaps that was the most "telling" piece of information when I thought about it. Young people who are in the first blush of love truly don't know each other. They don't know the best or the worst that each is capable of being. The princess certainly didn't know that her beloved would break his sacred promise to her, and he didn't know that his bride would endure hardship and danger to be with him.

So, when I put together all the information I had gathered, by researching, by considering the story, by telling it, and by talking about it, I had a completely different picture than I had when I started:

A prince (person with little power) made a promise that he had no right to make (usurped the right of his father) to a princess (person with no "real" power). He gave her a token (ring with royal seal?) of that promise. Then he made a promise to his father, the king (person with real power). The conflict between these two promises causes the princess to take an impossible action—she dresses up like a man, a hunter. Thereby empowered, she makes a journey (accompanied by eleven other women). She and the other women make up a powerful whole, a year. She does things she probably never thought she was capable of, and was therefore transformed, so when she came before this new king (person with power) she was not herself—that is, she was not the woman he thought he loved. She was a traveler (person with experiences) and a hunter (person with power). But there was one, a lion (other king, animal instincts) who saw the truth (because he had no preconceptions?). He convinced the king to test her, but there was another man (servant—limited power—different perspective) who "loved" these huntsmen. So the hunters/women pass the tests. Then, one day, another princess (person without power) shows up, and her appearance sets into motion the stripping away of pretenses. The king finally knows the truth of the woman he has promised to marry. And he acknowledges that truth by sending the "new" princess away, and by bringing back the lion, who is his alter-ego!

The end of the story is a moment of whimsy! I always love to say that last sentence, especially when I realized that the listener and the princess' attendants (and, I think, the king's servant who warned them) share a secret.

Knowing, or at least thinking that I know more about this remarkable story doesn't make it less wonderful. On the contrary, my delight in "The Twelve Huntsmen" increases every time I tell it! If you are interested in what all that work looks and sounds like, I tell this story on Volume 8 of the video, *The American Storytelling Series* (H. W. Wilson, 1986).

The Sack of Truth (Spanish)

In fairy tales, objects or animals can change shape and assist the protagonist. Sometimes there are magic spells, special words to say, but magic can be embodied in a totem, a kind of symbolic object, like a stick or a feather that has special powers. There is justice in a fairy tale, unlike in life. If a character in a fairy tale is kind to another person or animal, you can be sure that the kindness will be repaid. The following story is a composite: The first half concerns itself with the "three sons" motif. The second half has to do with marrying the princess (in this case, the Infanta), but it has less to do with the girl herself than with the King, who tries to "welch" on a promise. There is a charming variant in Richard Chase's collection, *The Jack Tales* (Houghton Mifflin, 1943).

THE STORY:

Many years ago, the King of Spain had a daughter. She was a beautiful little girl, and her father loved her. But when she turned sixteen, she became very sick. Doctors came from every corner of Spain, but none of them could cure the Infanta. So the king sent for the doctors of other countries. One by one they came until finally a doctor from Arabia examined her and said, "Send for the finest pears in Spain. If she eats three of the best pears in the land, she will recover." So the King ordered baskets and baskets of pears. Whoever could bring the pears that cured the Infanta would have his heart's desire. The King swore this by Santiago, the patron saint of Spain.

From all over the kingdom came men bringing baskets of pears— yellow pears and green ones, sweet pears and bitter ones. The Infanta wouldn't touch one bite.

In a small village lived a poor couple with three sons. Outside their little cottage grew a pear tree with the most delicious, fragrant, beautiful pears in all the land. So one day the father said to his oldest son, "Take some of the pears to the castle. Perhaps you can cure the King's daughter."

The oldest son set out on the road to the castle with his basket of pears, covered with a cloth. On the way he met a sad-faced woman with a child in her arms. "Where are you going, sir?" she asked.

"That's none of your business!" he snapped. "What does your basket hold?" she asked. "Horns!" was his reply. "Well then," she said, "Horns they shall be."

And when the oldest son got to the castle and offered his basket to the King, it was filled with horns. So the King threw him into the dungeon.

After a few days the poor man said to his second son, "Something must have happened to your brother. You must take a basket of pears to the castle and try your luck." So the second son did just as his brother had done. And as he walked on the road to the castle he came across that same woman with her babe.

"Where are you going, sir?" she asked. "None of your business!" he said. "And what does your basket hold?" "Stones!" he said, and he laughed at her. "Then stones they shall be," she said. And sure enough, when he got to the castle all the basket held was stones. And he, too, was thrown into the dungeon.

Now the third son was named Pedro, and when his two brothers did not return, he went to his father and asked for a basket to take some pears to the King. "My son, please don't go!" cried his father. "If neither of your brothers could cure the Infanta, how can you hope to succeed? And if you go, who will help your mother and me run the farm?" But the boy insisted, and he filled a basket with pears, covered it with a cloth, and set out on the road with his mother's tears and his father's blessing.

He came to a place where he met that same woman with the sad face. "Where are you going, sir?" she asked him. "Lady, I am going to the King's castle." "And what does your basket hold?" she asked. "Pears, to cure the Infanta." And then Pedro thought to himself, "I mustn't be greedy. After all, he who plays the fox for a day will pay for a year." And so he took a pear from the basket and held it out for the child.

The woman smiled and said, "Then, as you have said, let these be the pears that cure the Infanta! And since you were so generous, what would you have for yourself?" Pedro thought for a moment, and then he said, "I would like a whistle which will call to me any animal I choose when I blow it." The woman took a little silver whistle out of her pocket and handed it to Pedro. He thanked her, and hung the little whistle on a string around his neck. Then he went on to the castle.

When he got there, the King took one look at the pears, plump and golden and smelling so sweet, and he cried, "Why these must be the finest pears in the world!" He took them to the Infanta.

She ate one, and she sat up in bed. She ate two, and the color returned to her cheeks. She ate the third, and she jumped out of bed and danced a little dance! The King was overjoyed, and he said to Pedro, "What do you want? Just name it and it is yours!"

"I want my brothers," he said. And the King had them released. Then he said, "Is there anything else?" Pedro went out of the castle, to a place near the forest, and with his silver whistle he called a little hare to him. Then he took the hare back to the King and said, "Listen to me. I wish to travel for a year, but at the end of that time I shall return and ask for your daughter's hand in marriage. Take this hare and put a mark on him. Then let him go. When I come back I will call him to you again, and that will be a sign of honor between us, and a reminder to you of your promise."

Now the King did not want his daughter to marry this peasant, but he thought, "No one can call back a wild hare!" So out loud before the whole court he said, "I promise." And he put a mark on the hare, and let it go. And that hare ran straight back into the forest.

Pedro traveled the country for a year, and everywhere he went he used the little whistle to call all kinds of animals, large and small, fierce and gentle, and he used them to do good for others. At the end of the year he traveled to the castle of the King, and as he passed the forest he blew on the little whistle and called the hare to him. When the King saw him coming, he sent his advisor to try to bargain the hare away from Pedro, so he wouldn't have to keep his promise.

Pedro agreed to sell the hare for a sack of gold. Then, when the advisor was just out of sight, he blew the little whistle, and the hare came running back to him.

Then the King sent his chief minister to try to bargain the hare away from Pedro. This time Pedro sold it for two sacks of gold. But as soon as the chief minister reached the castle gates Pedro whistled the hare back. When the chief minister got back to the King he was afraid to tell what had happened. "He will only deal with the King," he said.

So the King himself went out to try to get the hare away. Pedro went with him to the shadow of a great tree. "Your majesty," he said, "I will let you have the hare for nothing. All you have to do is give it a big kiss." And he pointed to the hare.

Well, the King was most embarrassed, but he looked around to make sure no one was watching, and then he gave the hare a kiss, and Pedro gave it to him. Then he followed the King into the courtyard, where everyone was waiting, the advisors and the ministers, and the Infanta herself.

"Your majesty," said Pedro, "before all the court you made a promise to me. Now, I brought you that wild hare that you are holding. Will you keep your promise now, and marry me to your daughter?" The courtiers began to talk, and the King did not know what to do. Just then his chief advisor whispered, "Your majesty, take a big sack and tell him he must fill it up with truth! And then he can marry the Infanta." And that's just what the King did.

Pedro took the sack and opened it wide. "Your majesty, is it true that I brought a basket of pears to the castle?"

"Yes," said the King. "That's true."

"Truth, go into the sack!" And Pedro made a motion as if he was flinging it into the sack. "And isn't it true that my pears cured the Infanta?"

"Yes, that's true."

"Truth, go into the sack. King, didn't I give you a wild hare as a sign of a promise between us?"

"Yes," smiled the King, stroking the hare. "That's true."

"Truth, go into the sack. And King, isn't it true that, in order to get that hare away from me you . . ."

"Enough!" cried the King. "The sack is full!"

And so Pedro married the Infanta and they had two children; a girl and a boy. And it took them a whole lifetime to reach the end of their happiness.

THE WORK:

In working on this story, I didn't do a formal outline. Instead, I made a list of all the recognizable elements, and then went to various collections to read other stories with the same, well-known motifs. In some cases, the other tales were exactly parallel to this one. In other instances, the concept was the same, but the specifics differed.

The first large category, in the story's chronology, is the Tale Type 610, *Fruit cures the princess.* The first thing I noted about this particular story is the age of the princess, and the Spanish word for the daughter of a monarch—Infanta, the female baby. There are echoes of Catholicism in the title (and in the madonna-like figure of the woman who greets the three sons). The Infanta falls ill at a time when it might be guessed that she is becoming sexually aware. The nature of her illness is unspecified, and it is easy to imagine that she is "sick" in the same way that all adolescents or teens become restless or listless when their hormones begin to take over! It's no wonder that none of the doctors can cure her. Obviously, the situation in the story is more serious than a standard case of puberty, but that sexuality is certainly part of the subtext of the story.

So the stage is set for a classic promise: If you can cure my daughter, then you can marry her. After all, if the girl is going to die. . . . This promise, like many fairy tale vows, will have consequences! Whether it is the miller's daughter promising her firstborn child, or the king who promises half his kingdom, all promises are serious matters. They are the seeds of the conflict that will have to be resolved in one way or another!

The motif designation H346 refers to a test; in this case the test is that the Princess (or "your heart's desire," or whatever prize) will be given to the man who can heal her. The idea that pears, or any foods, have healing powers is an ancient one, and a current one! We still look to food to cure us. When we're feeling fussy or uncomfortable we instinctively think, "What do I want to eat?" as if making the right choice will eliminate that feeling of being out of balance—as well as the feeling of hunger. And, indeed, food can resolve feelings of longing or unease.

In many variants of this story the cure is effected with an apple—perhaps a reference to the fruit of knowledge that was eaten in the Garden of Eden. In fact, in the corresponding Grimm story (#165, "The Griffin") the fruit is an apple. In a story from China the restorative is a peach: for the Chinese this is a symbol of female sexuality. But the pear is particularly suggestive. It seems almost feminine in shape, and its texture is unlike that of any other fruit.

The next motif is L10, *Victorious youngest son*. There are three sons (or daughters) in European folk and fairy tales. In stories from other cultures, the significant number might be four or seven. But in this, as in practically every other three-sibling tale, it is the third child who is the child of fate. She or he might be the bravest, or the kindest (as in this case), or the most honest, or even the most foolish! But there is a quality about being the youngest, the most protected, the "baby" of the family, that invites a listener to empathize. Even if you are the oldest or the middle child, each one of us was, at one time, the youngest. We know what it means to be the closest to our parents. The youngest child is the representation of the underdog—we all root for him to be vindicated! In legal terms, the third child is frequently disenfranchised: "To the oldest child was left the mill, to the second child was left the donkey. But the youngest child got nothing but his father's old cat." These poor inheritances always end up being very valuable, at least in the stories!

Now, that sad woman on the path. . . . She seems to be very much a Madonna with child. It is interesting to note that she never actually asks for something. That fact makes the older brothers' actions even more outrageous. They are rude to her out of their own natures, not from a reaction to any request from her. When the third brother comes along, his simple sincerity is in stark contrast to the behavior of his brothers. Also, he alone has a name. In some versions of this or other three-sibling stories, the older boys are also named, and their names, like Pedro, are the Spanish equivalents of John Smith. In the folk and fairy tales of every culture, the names of the heroes are generally the most popular, ordinary names available. In the Jack Tales, Jack's older brothers are Tom and Will. And no one ever has a last name!

The magic transformation of the pears into horns and stones are, it seems, a case of "be careful what you wish for; you may get it" (Magic transformation motifs D400–499). When the older brothers lie, the woman changes their lies into the truth. It is a rather neat way of foiling them, because their own words are their downfall. When I tell the story the audience always becomes part of the telling at this point, because I say, "And when he got to the palace, what do you think his basket held?" Of course, listeners, especially children, always respond "Stones!" or "Horns!"

This moment of being tripped up by our own words—that happens to all of us when we speak without thinking. And naturally it is the youngest brother, who is himself so kind and so innocent that he cannot ascribe bad motives to anyone else, who speaks the truth. In one sense he tells the truth not because he is so virtuous, but because he cannot imagine that anyone else is venal. And he follows the advice of an old folk saying and offers a pear. And, as a blessing, the woman makes his words just as true as those of his brothers. This is fairly obvious, but the next piece is less so.

When offered a boon, Pedro makes a very specific request, and one that, up to now, has no connection to the rest of the story. In the Jack Tale variant, Jack knows that he has to control a wild rabbit, and his benefactor, an old man, gives him a drill to stick in the ground. In a Jewish variant, the hero finds a whistle lying on the ground, and that enables him to control the king's forty hares ("Forty Hares and a Princess," in *Yiddish Folktales*, edited by Beatrice Silverman Weinreich. Pantheon, 1988). The difference is that in this story the hero requests something that produces sound. Pedro asks for a whistle, and not just any whistle, but one that will control animals. The implication (at least in some Freudian circles) is that by controlling animals he can also control his own animal side. But it's still a curious request, especially given the lighthearted nature of this story, and when one tells the story it seems to come out of nowhere. It has the feeling of a clumsy setup for a joke that has yet to be played. I don't really have any better analysis of this motif, but I always felt that it was curious enough to stand on its own with an audience. No explanations are necessary or, perhaps, possible! This is just one of those fairy tale devices that you have to take on faith.

The next part of the story is fairly standard, expected plot exposition. The boy goes to the palace and fulfills his promise (and the promise of the woman, who is never seen again—as befits fairy godmothers or visions of the divine). Now the type changes to 570, *Herding the Hares*. The king's promise and the gift of the whistle collide when Pedro summons a hare! Every child can tell what is going to happen. In fact, once when I told the story and got to the point where Pedro "whistled up" the hare, one little boy said, "Uh-oh!" and everyone laughed. They laughed because the boy had voiced what we all knew: "Someone's going to be sorry!"

When our hero returns, the stage is set for the resolution. Here, the story has an awkward turn. The hare has been recalled, and yet the king still refuses to keep his promise. Pedro could, I reasoned, whistle the hare away from the king, but instead the focus of the "test" changes from the hare to filling the sack. There are a lot of examples of this kind of test, either filling the sack (or bowl, or box) with truth or lies. In the Jewish variant, first the king's advisor, then the queen, then the king (in disguise) all try to get the hare, and the young man has each one of them kiss the hare. Then he whistles it back. But the catch here is that he instructs the king to kiss the hare "under his tail." ("Beneath its scut," in the original language.) Now, that is an action that might well be perceived to be so embarrassing that the king would rather concede his daughter than have it known! In fact, after having found this version, when I tell the Spanish variant, I indicate the hare's hind end by miming lifting his tail. Children are, I hardly need to mention, delighted by this turn of events, and it makes the end much more logical.

The final moment of the story, the thought with which the listener is left, is a formula end-phrase. It is an elegant end to this tale of honesty and humor. The phrase even feels good in the teller's mouth: "And it took them a whole lifetime to reach the end of their happiness." It seems to me almost like a benediction, as if the story is saying, "We all deserve a lifetime of happiness." It's a very satisfying end to a story that embodies many traditional fairy-tale concepts.

The Silent Princess (Jewish)

This multi-layered story (with internal stories that emphasize the conflicts of the larger tale) comes from the Jewish tradition, although the motifs can be found in stories from Denmark, Poland, and India, among others. The version I tell is adapted from a story in Howard Schwartz's book, *Elijah's Violin*, and two variants in *Jewish Folktales* by Pinhas Sadeh (106–112). There is a charming version (more appropriate for children) in *Thirteen Danish Tales*, retold by Mary Hatch. The riddles in the inner stories are similar to those found in dozens of "dilemma tales," but there is an element of choice in this story that is special and particular.

THE STORY:

There was once a young man from a good family, who studied all the learned and sacred books until one day he went to his father and said, "Father, I would like your permission to travel and see the world. I think there must be more to life than one can learn from books." His father said, "You are right, my son. There is more to life than one can learn from books. Go. Travel. But please don't stay away too long. Promise that you will return to me in one year." The young man promised, and then he left.

He traveled through different lands until he came to a certain kingdom. The king of this land had one daughter, and she was very beautiful. The king should have been happy, but there was a problem. The princess hadn't spoken a single word in her entire life. Not one! The king called on physicians from all over the world, but it was no use. Now some said the princess could not speak, that she was sick. And some said that the princess could speak if she wished. And the king didn't know what to believe. But he sent out word that he would give the princess in marriage to anyone who could get the girl to speak. But if any man tried and failed, he would be put to death. Many came, and many tried, for the princess was most beautiful. But they all failed, and one by one they paid with their heads.

Now, when the young man heard that he thought, "Why would anyone risk his life for a girl?" Then he looked at the palace, and his eyes wandered up and up, until there, in a window halfway up the palace wall, he saw the loveliest face he had ever seen. Right away he went to the king. "Your Majesty," he said, "I wish to speak with your daughter." The king looked at him for a moment. "You know the price if you fail?" The young man said, "Yes, I know."

So that night the young man was shown to the princess' chambers, and there sat the princess, and there a witness to see if she should speak. Then the doors were closed and locked. The young man walked right up to where the princess was sitting and he said . . . nothing! Not one word! One hour he stood before her. Three hours he stood, and still not a word. And the princess thought, "How strange. All the other men have questioned me, or shouted at me, or insulted me, and this man says nothing."

Well, after a long time the young man turned to the witness and said, "Well, it's going to be a long night. Let us pass the time telling stories." But the witness said, "No. I am a witness. I am here to watch and to listen, not to tell stories."

"Fine," said the young man. "Well, if I ask you a question, will you answer it?" "Maybe I will," said the witness, "and maybe I won't." "Fine!" said the young man, and he proceeded to tell this story.

"You see," he said, "three men went traveling together: a tailor, a carpenter, and a maggid (a wandering preacher). They traveled for a long time until night, when they came to a dark forest. So they decided to stop and spend the night. And because they feared the wild beasts of that place, they decided that each man should keep watch, one at a time. First it was the carpenter's turn. He watched, shivering in the dark, until he happened to see a piece of wood, a log, lying there. So, just to keep himself awake, he got out his tools and began to carve. And he worked until he had carved a little girl-doll. Then he saw that his time was up, and he woke the tailor. When the tailor saw this little doll that the carpenter had made, he thought it was so perfect that it should have clothes! So he took out his own tools, and he began to sew. He sewed a complete set of clothes for the little girl—everything she needed! And when he dressed her, she looked just perfect! Then he saw that his watch was up, so he nudged the maggid. When the maggid saw this little girl-doll, he was so amazed! It looked so real that he decided, 'Something this perfect ought to be alive!' So he began to pray. And he called upon the Holy One, Blessed Be He, to fill this thing with the breath of life! And as he prayed the little doll grew. And when the first rays of the sun's light touched it, that little doll-girl drew breath and was alive!

"At that moment the other men woke up and as soon as they saw her they began to argue, over whose girl she was. 'She belongs to me,' said the carpenter. 'I carved her and made her look real.' 'No, she belongs to me,' said the tailor. 'I dressed her and made her look human.' 'Ah, she belongs to me,' said the maggid, 'for I caused the Holy One to fill her with the breath of life, without which she would still have been just a wooden doll, no matter how well carved or how beautifully dressed.' And they continued to argue like that. Now I ask you," said the young man to the witness, "To whom does she belong?"

And the poor witness, she thought and thought, but finally she said, "I don't know. I'll ask a judge in the morning." "In the morning! In the morning it's going to be too late for me!" said the young man. "Couldn't you think of an answer now?" And from across the room came, "The maggid." "I beg your pardon?" said the young man. "She belongs to the maggid," said the princess. "Really?" said the young man. "Why is that?"

"Because he called upon the Holy One to fill her with life. He brought life into her, without which she would have just been a piece of wood. She belongs to the maggid."

The young man gazed at her for a moment. Then he said softly, "Thank you. I'm sure you're right." And then, to the witness, "Now let's all get some sleep!" In the morning the guards came to drag the young man out to his executioner, but the witness said, "No, no! She spoke! I heard her!" And all eyes turned to the princess who said . . . nothing. The king looked from the young man to his daughter and back. But he didn't know what to do. So he decided to give the young man a second evening.

That night the young man was shown into the princess' chambers, and there sat the princess, and there two witnesses, to see if she should speak. Then the doors were closed and locked. The young man walked right up to where the princess was sitting and he said . . . nothing! Two hours. Four hours went by, and finally the young man went to the two witnesses and said, "Well, it's going to be a long night. Let us pass the time telling stories." But the witnesses said, "No. We are witnesses. We are here to watch and to listen, not to tell stories."

"Fine," said the young man. "Well, if I ask you a question, will you answer it?" "Maybe we will," said the witnesses, "and maybe we won't." "Fine!" said the young man, and he proceeded to tell this story.

"Well," he said, "three people were traveling together: a lord, and his lady, and the coachman. Well, they drove on and on until they came to a place where they were set upon by bandits. They cut off the lord's head. They cut off the coachman's head. They took all their money and then they left the lady there to mourn. And the poor lady wept and wept and tore her hair and tore her clothes. And she wept until there were no more tears left in her. By that time it was very dark, and after a while, when she was quiet, the lady heard two voices in the tree above her! Two blackbirds were talking.

'Tsk, tsk! Look at that! The lord and the coachman with their heads off!' 'Yes,' said the second, 'and the lady is very sad. It's too bad.' 'Yes it's too bad she doesn't know about this tree. If she only knew,' said the first blackbird, 'she could take some of the leaves from the tree, pound them into a pulp, squeeze the juice over the two mens' heads, and they would be good as new. Too bad she doesn't know. Tsk, tsk, tsk.'

"When she heard that the lady jumped to her feet and tore some of the leaves from the tree. She placed the two heads next to the two bodies, squeezed the juice over them, and the two men stood up as good as ever! But, as the light of the sun shone over them she could see that she'd placed the lord's head on the coachman's body, and the coachman's head on the lord's body, and now the two men began to argue over whose wife was she anyway!

'She is my wife,' said the lord's head on the coachman's body. 'This is the face she married.' 'No, She is my wife,' said the coachman's head on the lord's body. 'This is the body she sleeps with!' And they went on and on in this fashion.

"Now," said the young man to the witnesses, "To whom was the lady married?" And the two witnesses, well, they thought, and they thought, and they fussed and they fumbled. And finally they said, "We don't know. We'll ask a wise man in the morning."

"In the morning!" said the young man, "In the morning it's going to be too late for me! Couldn't you think of an answer now?" And from across the room came a soft voice, "She belongs to the lord's head on the coachman's body."

The young man turned to the princess. "Why is that?" "Because," said the princess, "in that head is all loving, all caring, all remembrance, all choosing." She smiled. "She belongs to the lord's head on the coachman's body." The young man went over to her, and held out his hand, and the princess placed her hand in his. And they sat like that all night long. In the morning, when the doors were unlocked, no one had to ask. The two were married that day. And one year later the young man kept his promise to his father, and he took his wife back home with him. They lived many long years. They had children and grandchildren, and they spent many happy evenings together, just talking.

THE WORK:

This story has always proved very controversial, both for me when I first read it and for listeners whenever I tell it. The one word that grates on many modern ears is "belong." To whom does she belong? The question itself seems offensive to modern women, and yet belonging is at the very heart of what this story is about. The word "belong" has several thesaurus entries. "Be a member, have place, pertain to, relate to." Under "have place" is "fit" or "fit in." Under "relate to" you find "associate, connect, ally, link, wed, bind, . . ." So, now it seems more and more that the state of belonging is something that can be seen in a positive light. The modern woman says, "I belong to no one. I belong to myself!" The woman of the Middle East, and of the middle ages, says, "I belong to and with my husband. And by belonging, I have a place in the world." If this concept does not make the story valuable, if the teller doesn't love the story, then that teller shouldn't tell it.

There is another element of this story that is intriguing. The story is about silence and speech. Therefore, it seemed very important to me that the words be chosen with extreme care. So I looked at the patterns of the story and of the internal riddles. The riddle stories serve two different purposes: first, they are a familiar device for this culture group. Original audiences would have been caught up in the dilemma. They might have offered their own opinions about the justice of the decisions! But the riddles have another purpose. They reinforce the theme of belonging and of choice. In the first riddle, the three men create a life (with the help of God) and they are responsible for that life. The arguments have to do with the nature of that life they have made. Is humanity embodied in how we look? If so, then the block of wood, perfectly carved, would have been alive.

Is humanity determined by fashion? If so, then the clothes would have made her alive. But the riddle (at least as it is solved in this version) implies that life is divine. And according to the logic of the riddle, the maggid, as a kind of stand-in for the Creator, has responsibility for this life.

The second riddle is about what constitutes marriage. If marriage has to do with appearances, then she belongs to the lord's head on the coachman's body. If a marriage is merely sex, then she would belong to the coachman's head and the lord's body. But the solution to the riddle seems to say that marriage, and love, and belonging have to do with shared experiences, and with choosing. (One version of the story also says, "and the head can be seen by all," but that seems somehow less convincing.) The element of knowledge and memory is what differentiates one person from another. Even identical twins have some separate experiences.

It is important to note here that in the versions that I was able to locate there is one additional riddle, one additional evening in the pattern. In telling the story, I felt that the additional riddle ("Who Cured the Princess?") was less effective than the others, and telling it simply took too much time, so I chose to eliminate it. Also, if you were to look at other versions, you would find that they are more skeletal than mine. In working on the story, I took several indications of speech, and turned them into dialogue. (In other words, I turned, "He asked to speak with the princess," into "He said, 'Your majesty, I wish to speak with your daughter.'")

Apart from these changes, I found the story a strange mix of appealing and off-putting. It's important to find out exactly what attracts you to a particular story. You may never know for sure, but the search is worth the effort. For me, this story was about choice, power, coercion, and love. So the way I have chosen to tell it reflects my sensibilities. For one thing, the young man is free in the world. That is, he doesn't "belong" to anyone. In modern parlance he is unattached! The princess is, to the contrary, the possession of her father (in Middle Eastern society). But within the confines of her world she has accomplished something very substantial: she has managed to choose her own fate. That is, through the device of her silence, she has manipulated her situation. That is remarkable!

The last moment of the story is mine—pure invention. When I tell the story there are certain elements that cannot be transferred to the page. For some tellers, the story is about trickery. The young man presents a puzzle, and the poor princess is tricked into speaking. And other versions or variants of the story make that trick the point of the story. The implication is not only insulting (the poor princess couldn't keep her mouth shut?), but also seems to be inconsistent with the facts of the story; that is, the princess has had many suitors, but has never spoken. I cannot imagine that she could be fooled into a response. It seems, rather, that she is invited to respond. The young man essentially goes only halfway toward a union with her. The princess must come the rest of the way herself. By telling stories instead of using the kinds of tactics that others had used, shouting or demanding answers, the young man presents her with a choice. He opens a door to a partnership. And that is exactly what storytelling is about. It is a partnership between the teller and the listener. We agree to enter into an act of creation that is every bit as impressive as that of the three travelers in each story within this story. We make a choice.

This version is substantially altered from the other written versions I have named. I have carefully selected certain phrases, and repeated them. I have left out one riddle, and I have "personalized" the characters in the way that I tell the story. Those are the choices I have made as the teller. I take responsibility for those choices, which I made only after locating several variants, and doing the kind of work that is outlined above. The story still upsets some listeners, and I pay attention to what they say, because every time the story is told, it is the first time for someone.

The Grateful Crane (Japanese)

In this story, kindness is repaid with a magical gift. This is a classic fairy tale, and one that is as universally known in Japan as *Beauty and the Beast* or *Cinderella* are in Western countries. One cultural note: in Japan, cranes are considered good omens, symbols of creativity and fertility.

THE STORY:

There was once a very poor old couple who lived alone in a tiny house far from the village. They had no children, and the old man made his living by gathering sticks of wood for firewood, and selling them in the marketplace.

One day he was on his way to the village when it began to snow. Before long everything was covered with snow, making great white shapes all around. Suddenly he saw something strange in the middle of a field. Something was fluttering and churning up the snow.

"Why, what's this?" he thought to himself. "It looks like a little snowstorm in the middle of the field."

But when he got closer he could see that it was a crane, with its leg caught in a trap. "Poor thing," he said, and he bent over it to free it. "Here, here. Don't struggle so. You're getting all tangled up in the rope." And gently he freed the bird.

As soon as it was free, the crane flew off into the sky, but before it left, it circled over the old man's head three times.

"Good bye! Good luck!" he called to it, and he watched until it was just a speck in the sky. It seemed to him that the crane was a good omen. Then he picked up his bundle of wood, and went to the village. In the marketplace he sold all his wood, and then he went back to his little home.

When he got there he told his wife what had happened. "You did a good thing, my husband. A kind thing. And I would have done the same." And the two old people thought about the crane flying free over the mountains.

Just then there was a tapping at the door. "Now who could be out on a night like this?" the old man wondered. Then he heard a gentle voice. "Gomen kudasai? Is anyone home?"

The old woman hurried to the door and opened it, and there stood a slender woman, all dressed in white, and covered with snow.

"Come in, come in," said the old woman. "You must be half frozen."

The young woman came in and shook the snow from her shoulders. "Thank you. It is so cold outside." Her cheeks were red and her hands were icy cold. "I was traveling to visit some friends, and I got lost in the snow," she said. "May I stay here for the night?"

"I'm so sorry," said the old woman, "but we are very poor and we have no quilts for you to sleep on."

"Oh, that's all right," said the woman. "I don't need any quilts. Whatever you have will be good enough."

"And I can only offer you some rice and soup," added the old man.

"Whatever you are eating will be good enough for me. Please do not worry. I am grateful just to be inside." And with that the young woman went into the kitchen where the old woman was fixing dinner.

"Let me help you," said the beautiful young woman, and she worked quickly and quietly to fix dinner and serve it to the old couple. When they were done she gathered up the bowls and washed them without saying a word.

"You are a good and a kind child," the old man and the old woman said as they wished her good night. The next morning, when they awoke, they found that she was already awake, and had prepared breakfast for them. And she stayed with them another day, and another, and another. Before too long they were treating her like a daughter. It seemed that she had always been there. And she was as sweet and as gentle to them as if she was indeed their child.

One day the girl said, "I would like to give you something to make your life easier. Go to the village and get me a loom and some thread." The old man went, and he brought back a small loom and as much beautiful, colored thread as he could afford.

"Now," said the girl, "I am going to weave something for you. But you must promise not to enter my room while I am weaving." And she took the thread and the loom into her little room, and they could hear the sound of the loom as she wove. For three days and nights she worked, not even stopping to eat. At the end of that time she opened the door. When they saw her they were so worried! She looked pale and tired, and she could hardly stand without help. "Here," she said. "Now you can sell this in the marketplace." And she handed the old man a most remarkable piece of embroidered cloth! It was snow white, with silver and white cranes flying everywhere. It was the most exquisite cloth the old man and his wife had ever seen!

"It is too beautiful to sell!" exclaimed the old man.

"Never mind," the girl said. "I want you to sell it and buy anything you want. It is all I have to give you for your kindness to me." And she went into her room and lay down, exhausted, and slept.

So the old man took it to the marketplace, where a wealthy man looked at it with wonder. "This is the finest piece of cloth I have ever seen!" And he paid a great deal of money for it. The old man hurried home with good things to eat, presents for his wife and the girl, and still enough money to live on for many weeks. And they were all very happy until, once more, times grew hard and the money had almost run out.

"Father," the girl said sweetly, "Take the last money and buy me some thread." And he did. Once more the girl went into her room. Three days and three nights she worked, and when she came out she was holding a piece of cloth even more beautiful than the last. And again, the old man took the cloth to the marketplace and sold it for a whole sack of money.

It took the girl two days to recover from weaving this cloth, but now they had enough money to keep them very comfortably for many weeks. But time went by, and the money slowly ran out. For a third time the old man bought thread, and the girl went into her room to weave.

This time the old woman could hardly stand it. "Husband," she said, "how does she weave and embroider such magnificent cloth?" "I don't know," said the man, "but we promised not to look."

"Oh, just one little peek! What harm could that be?" And she tiptoed to the door and slid it open.

But instead of the girl, there, standing at the loom, was a great white crane. It was plucking out its own breast feathers, and weaving them into extraordinary cloth!

"Ojiii-san! Ojii-san!" cried the old woman, running back to her husband. And she told him what she had seen. The old man was so sad. "I told you not to look," he said, shaking his head. And the two of them waited to see what would happen.

At the end of three days and three nights the girl emerged, so pale that you could almost see through her skin to her bones. And she carried a piece of cloth more beautiful and delicate than the first two. "I am the crane that you freed in the snowstorm," she said to the old man. "Do you remember me? I wanted to repay you, so I took this form so that I could help you. But now that you know what I am, I must leave you."

They wept and begged her to stay, but she said, "Don't worry. I promise that you will never have to work hard again. And whenever you see a crane, you will remember me. Thank you for saving my life!" Then she stepped outside, and once more she became a beautiful white crane, right before their eyes. She lifted her great wings and rose into the sky, with the moon glinting off her wings. She circled their house three times, before flying off toward the mountains.

The old couple was lonely without her, but they were never poor or hungry again. And they always remembered their crane-daughter.

THE WORK:

The act of transformation (Motifs D0–D799) is one key motif in fairy tales, and in this story it is the central element. There is an initial act of kindness that is repaid. The story is very straightforward about the message that it intends to impart. So the only questions are why and how does transformation take place, and what does it mean when it occurs.

Japanese culture is respectful of the elderly, so this story is not only entertaining. It also repeats (indoctrinates, you might say) a societal and cultural lesson. And the "conduit" for this respect is a magical creature: a crane/daughter. In order to properly understand the affection and esteem that the Japanese people feel for the crane, one has to picture them in flight. They have a huge wingspan, and the appellation "little snowstorm" gives you a feeling for how impressive a sight they must be.

Now, the crane returns to the old couple for two reasons: First, to repay the old man's kindness. The second reason is cultural. In Japan, a childless couple is an object of pity or scorn. When I stopped to think about it, I wondered why it was a daughter, a female crane. Well, perhaps it has something to do with the responsibilities of sons versus daughters. In Japanese society, both sexes are responsible for taking care of parents, but daughters would have to leave the parental home when they marry. Sons are more likely to live in (and inherit) their parents' home. So, why is this crane female? Since there is no definitive answer, it is open to speculation—and I, as the storyteller, can make a choice for my own telling. Is it because daughters are better care-givers? Or kinder? More likely, it's because of the kinds of domestic chores that women perform, and because in Japanese society, as in others, daughters stay home until they marry, but sons may travel. (On the other hand, sons return to care for their parents after they marry, because sons inherit, but daughters do not. Ask enough questions and you come up with more questions!)

Then I thought about the miracle that allows this crane/daughter to weave such rare cloth. Weaving is a particularly female task in Japan. Men may prepare the yarn, but only women weave. Still, that doesn't explain why the crane is female. But weaving is an act of creation, and in this case it comes from the body of the crane. The story says that the family had nothing. And women can create something out of their own bodies. As a teller, that is the most remarkable piece of this story. The creation of something wondrous out of the crane's own body, that is the pivotal point of the story. She takes her own feathers/flesh—at great expense and pain—and creates something of beauty and value. If that isn't a description of childbirth, what is?

So, I think to myself, this is a story about filial devotion that goes on even to the next generation. The crane/daughter pays her parents back for the gift of her life. She does it with service and she does it with the gifts of her own body. So the cloth is sold to provide for the old ones. But they break the taboo, and have to release their daughter to go back to her own fate (marriage?). The three cloths, each woven in three days, are a typical case of number-magic. There is no hard-and-fast definitive meaning for the number, but it is common enough to be familiar to the listener.

When I tell the story I feel that the moment of exposing her secret is a very delicate one. If I am too "precious" about it, then it becomes comical. If I don't give the moment its proper weight, then I am guilty of backing away from the miracle. This is the moment of the telling for which all the work is preparation. After this moment, the rest of the story is just winding down.

This may not be a definitive interpretation, but it is thorough enough to give me a solid footing for telling and that, after all, is the purpose of all this work!

Dorani (Indian/Lang)

This story, like *The Silent Princess*, relates to themes of choice, love, and—curiously enough—silence. however, in the case of this story from the Punjab region of India, I had to use different methods, much more subjective choices, primarily because I could only locate one written version, although there are similar motifs in other fairy tales.

THE STORY:

There was once a merchant, a seller of perfumes, who had a daughter, and her name was Dorani. It so happened that this girl had a friend who was a fairy maiden, and the two of them were much loved and valued by the fairy king, the Rajah Indra. Every night they would travel to his palace in the forest, and there a magical lute would play without a touch of human or fairy hand, and the two girls would sing and dance until dawn.

Dorani had the most lovely, long hair, the color of spun gold, and it hung all down her back. One hot day it felt so heavy to her that she cut off a few inches, wrapped the locks in a huge leaf, and threw it into the stream that ran just below her window. Now, it so happened that that same stream ran through the place where the king's son had gone to hunt. When he went to the stream to drink, he saw the leaf float by, and from it he could smell the most exquisite odor, like roses! The king's son waded into the stream and caught up the leaf, and when he opened it, he saw a lock of hair the color of the sun!

When the king's son returned home, he was so quiet and sad that his father the king could not help but notice. The young man didn't eat, and he couldn't sleep. Finally his father said, "My son, what has happened to you? Are you ill? Is there anything I can do to help you?" The young prince didn't say a word, but reached inside his shirt and removed a leaf, and he handed that to his father. The king unfolded the leaf, and there was the most remarkable lock of hair, golden, and with a faint scent of roses. "Father," said the prince, "if I do not win and marry the maid that owns that lock of hair, then I will surely die!"

So the king sent out his heralds throughout all his kingdom to search for the maiden with the hair like spun gold. The word went out, and Dorani heard it in the marketplace. She spoke to her father and said, "Father, if it is my hair, then I must do what the king commands. But I beg you, go to the king and tell him that I am willing to marry his son if I may have one favor. I will spend every day at the palace, but every night I must spend in my old home."

Her father listened with amazement, but he knew that his daughter was very wise, so he said nothing. Sure enough, after a while the messengers discovered that the lock of hair did indeed belong to Dorani, and her father was summoned to the palace.

When he came to the palace, the perfume-seller told the king what his daughter had said. "Your majesty, we must obey you in all things, but the maid asks only this one thing. That she be permitted to return to her father's house each night." The king was much amazed by this, but his son was willing, and after all it was their own business. He thought that the girl would tire of it very soon, so he made no difficulty, and the wedding was arranged quickly.

At first the young prince thought nothing about it. His bride was beautiful, and he would have her with him all day. But he was very disturbed to find that his bride sat upon a low stool all day long, with her forehead on her knees, and she would not talk to him. He spoke gently to her, thinking she was afraid, but Dorani simply sat like a stone all day, without uttering a word. Then each evening, at dusk, she rose and went to the street where there was a palanquin waiting to take her back to her father's house, and each morning, at dawn, she would return. But not a word would she speak. She wouldn't even look at her husband when he spoke to her.

Now the prince began to despair, and he grew sadder and sadder. One day, when he was walking in his garden he met the old gardener, who had been his friend since he was a child. The old man looked at him and said, "Child, my prince, why are you so troubled?" The prince told his old friend his story. "I have married a woman who is as beautiful as the stars, but she won't speak to me, and I don't know what to do. Night after night she leaves to go to her father's house, and day after day she sits as if turned to stone. No matter what I do or say, she won't utter a word, and I am at my wit's end."

The old man thought for a moment, then went into his cottage. When he returned he handed the prince some small packets of paper. "Your majesty, tomorrow, when your bride leaves, sprinkle some of the powder in these packets over you and you will become invisible. That is all I can do to help you, but it may be enough."

The prince thanked him, and rushed back to the palace. That night, when Dorani arose and went to the street, the prince took one packet out and sprinkled the powder over himself. Sure enough, he became invisible! He rushed out into the street, just in time to follow the palanquin to Dorani's father's house. There Dorani went through the first door and removed one veil. She went through another doorway and removed a second veil. When she came to her chambers, she removed the last veil. In her room was a basin of rose-water. Dorani called for some food, and then she washed her hair in the rose-scented water. She dressed in her most beautiful robe, and wound ropes of pearls around her waist, and roses in her hair. Then she sat upon a large stool that was hung with a canopy and spoke these words: "Fly, stool, at my command! Fly to the palace of Rajah Indra!" And instantly the stool rose in the air! The prince barely had time to grab onto one of the legs of the stool before he was whisked out of the window and over the town. They soon arrived at the home of Dorani's friend. "Have you spoken to your husband?" asked the girl. "The stool is flying all crooked!" But Dorani said she hadn't said a word to him, and soon the stool was in the air again, and they were on their way to the palace of the fairy rajah, Indra.

All night long they sang and danced, and the magic lute played, and through it all the prince sat, entranced at the sight of his wife. When morning was approaching, Indra gave the signal for the music to cease, and the two girls sat down once more upon the magic stool. The prince clung to the leg of the stool, and was carried back to the perfume-seller's house. He just had time to rush back to his own house, where he became visible again. So he lay down on his couch and waited for Dorani.

When she arrived, Dorani went to her seat, as usual, and sat with her head upon her knees. For a while not a word was said by either of them. Then the prince said, "I had such a strange dream last night. I know you won't speak to me, but as it was about you, I shall tell you about it." And he proceeded to tell his wife exactly what he had seen the night before. As she listened to him, Dorani was curious, and filled with wonder. "Could it be," she thought to herself, "that he really dreamed all this?" But she said not a word. She only looked up at him once, and then put her head down again.

The next night the same thing happened. The prince followed, invisible, and clung to the leg of the stool, which flew even more unsteadily. And when they returned home, he told her everything that he had seen, pretending it was a dream. When he was finished Dorani gazed at him and said, "Is it true that you dreamed it all, or were you there?"

"I was there," he answered.

"Why do you follow me?" she demanded.

"Because," replied the prince, "I love you, and to be with you is all my happiness."

Dorani said nothing for the rest of the day, but sat silently with her head down. But in the evening, when she was preparing to leave she turned to him and said, "If you love me, don't follow me tonight." And although it was difficult, the prince did as she asked and stayed at home.

That evening the stool flew so crazily that the two girls could scarcely stay upon it. "Are you certain you didn't speak to your husband?" demanded the other girl. "The stool flies like it never has before." "Yes," Dorani admitted, "I spoke to him."

That night the two girls danced and sang more magnificently than ever. Dorani was so marvelous that in the end the Rajah Indra stood and swore that he would give her any present she wished. At first she would not ask for anything, but after he pressed her she said, "Give me the magic lute." When the Rajah heard that he was very annoyed. "Take it then!" he said. "But you must never come here again, for I have nothing better to give you, and you'll never be satisfied with other gifts!"

Dorani bowed her head, and took the lute silently. Then the two were transported back to their homes. Dorani returned to the prince's palace, where he was waiting. But this day, she sat upon her seat, and after a while she said, "Did you dream again last night?" And he laughed with joy. "No, I did not dream last night. But I begin to dream now. Not of the past, but of what might be in the future."

That day Dorani sat very quietly, but when her husband spoke to her, she answered him. And when evening came she still sat. "Are you not going to your father's house, Dorani?" And she rose and embraced him. "Never, my husband, will I leave thee!"

That is how the prince won his beautiful bride. (adapted by the author from Andrew Lang's *The Olive Fairy Book*)

THE WORK:

This story, like *The Silent Princess*, has very sexual overtones. In addition, it deals in very similar ways with issues of control and choice. But these stories "feel" as if they come from different cultures, which of course, they do. The Aarne-Thompson Tale Type is 306A, *The Princess Who Danced in Heaven*, and it is listed in D. L. Ashliman's book, along with two variants.

There is one point that I had changed when I first told the story. In the original, as in my adaptation, the "girl friend" is a fairy maiden. I have sometimes eliminated that reference because I wanted to make a clear line between the fairy world, and the everyday world of the marketplace and home and palace. When I thought about it in relation to this volume, I was forced to rethink and re-rethink these choices. Although I sometimes believe that this fairy maiden seems out of place in the daytime world, the other factor is that she is the link, the connection with that night-time world. And a friend pointed out that when Dorani answers her friend by "admitting" that she spoke to her husband, there is a conscious choice to sever that link. In that moment—not in the time with her husband—Dorani redefines her relationship with the fairy world and with her husband's world.

The language is wonderful, and the list of interesting words includes:

Dorani—The last part of the name indicates a princess. So this girl, although born to a seller of scents is, at her core, royalty. I found it interesting that only one person in this story rates a name. The fairy Rajah Indra is well known in Indian folklore.

Rajah Indra—The name "Indra" comes up in other contexts. In Vedic mythology he was the god of weather, controlling the rain. Later, he gets "downgraded" to the position of a minor demigod. He is frequently mentioned as being involved in mischief.

palanquin—A covered chair that is carried by way of poles. It would probably have had a curtain, behind which the passenger would be invisible to the people in the street. (Just as the prince was invisible to her.)

essence (or, in the original, attar) of roses—The essence of anything is important. The value of roses was probably very high. Perfumes were always a mark of wealth.

After considering all the above, here are some of the questions I asked.

• *Why hair?* Because of the very sexual nature of the image? Because it is an extension of her? It is hers, a part of her body, and yet she can cast it off.

• *Why is the story so specific about the odor of Dorani's hair?* Is it simply because of the use of perfume would mark her as either royalty or the daughter of someone who could afford certain luxuries? The sense of smell is so strong in most people that it can far outweigh hearing or even sight. The prince falls in love with the smell of her, transmitted through her hair (which is a very female and very sensual attribute). Also,

• *Why is her hair "the color of spun gold"?* Is this phrase true to the original, or does it come from the European filter through which the story has come to us? There are no indigenous blond people in India; in fact, blond hair is not considered particularly beautiful in India. So does this reference indicate her beauty (or rareness?) in Asian or in European terms? I must assume that this image comes from the collector, Major Campbell, and not from the native Indian teller, unless this was a case of the teller suiting his tale to the audience!

• *Why does the prince resort to the device of telling her his "dream"?* Is it because the events really do have a dreamlike quality about them? One can fly in a dream, but not in reality. Freudian psychology equates flying with sexual experience. By flying, the prince enters into her world, instead of insisting that she remain in his. Also, he uncovers a secret. But instead of confronting her, he allows her to maintain her world (fantasy) until she is ready to give it up and enter his world (reality).

There is also a question of maturity. Just as in "The Twelve Huntsmen," the prince here forms a union without being aware of the consequences. He agrees to allow her to go back to her father's house (childhood) every night. Night, of course, is the time for consummating a marriage, but she spends it in a dream-like world. So both she and the prince have to make choices: Do they wish to leave behind their child-hoods (dreams, fairy land) to become a real couple with, as the prince says, a future'?'

There is a moment in the telling that I like a lot: just before she asks, "Did you dream this, or were you there?" I pause to give Dorani the time to think about the Prince's story, and then I ask the question very quietly. After all, these are the first words she has ever spoken to him! This section of the story is quiet, intimate. When the other maiden says to Dorani, "Did you speak to your husband?" Dorani answers in a slightly distracted fashion—she has other things on her mind. So the relationship between the first half of the story (setting out the facts of the meeting, the resolution of the first "problem"—locating the woman with this extraor-dinary hair and arranging the marriage) and the second half (new problem—getting her to speak/stay, the blossoming of love, understand-ing, caring) is like the relationship between fact and spirit. The first section is almost political; the second half is an emotional tightrope, like love.

Vassilissa and Baba Yaga (Russian)

In Russian oral fairy tales, these two characters are perhaps the most famous! There are several "Vassilissa" stories in Aleksandr Afanas'ev's collection *Russian Fairy Tales* (Random House, 1973), and "Grandmother Witch," Baba Yaga, shows up in dozens of tales. Vassilissa might be called a Russian Cinderella, for she is frequently portrayed as the only child of a widower, who then marries a widow with one or two other daughters. Baba Yaga is that most recognizable of fairy-tale characters, The Witch. In *Funk & Wagnalls Standard Dictionary of Folklore, Mythology, and Legend*, she is described as "a cannibalistic ogress, who steals and cooks her victims. . . ." Vassilissa and Baba Yaga meet in several fairy tales, but the following story is a composite. The beginning of "Vassilissa the Beauti-ful" is joined to the end of a story that, in the Afanas'ev version, is simply called "Baba Yaga." This is how I heard the story originally—I don't know if it exists in print like this, but it is so like other stories of this genre that I wanted to transcribe it as I tell it.

THE STORY:

In a certain tsardom there was a merchant who had one daughter who was called Vassilissa the Beautiful. When Vassilissa was eight years old, her mother took sick. As she felt her time draw near she called her daughter to her bed and said, "Now listen to me, my dearest child, and remember my words. Soon I will die, but I leave you my blessing, and this little doll. Keep her near you always, show her to no-one. If you ever have troubles, just feed the doll and ask her advice, and she will take care of you." Then she kissed her child, gave her the doll, and died.

The merchant mourned for a proper time, and then he began to think about marrying again. He chose a widow who was not young, but she was a good housekeeper, and she had two daughters that were about Vassilissa's age. So he married her. But this new wife was not a good mother for Vassilissa. She gave her very little food, and all the hardest work to do, and let her own daughters do nothing. She hoped that Vassilissa would grow thin and ugly and sunburned. But instead, Vassilissa grew more and more beautiful, while her own daughters grew thin and bitter with spite! And how was this possible? Well, the doll helped Vassilissa with all her work. Every night, when the others were asleep, Vassilissa would take out the little doll and feed her whatever crumbs she had been given that day. Then when the doll was finished, Vassilissa would say, "Oh, my little doll, I have such troubles!" The doll listened, then she would say, "Don't worry my Vassilissa. Sleep well. The morning is wiser than the evening."

Now years passed, and Vassilissa was old enough to marry. Many suitors came to ask for her hand, but they didn't even glance at the two older girls. And their mother was furious, and sent them all away saying, "We will not wed the youngest until the older have been wed!" And as every day went by, Vassilissa grew more and more beautiful, and the other two grew more bitter and ugly!

One day the merchant had to leave his home for a long time to trade in a distant city. The stepmother moved with the three girls to a house that was near a deep forest. In that forest there was a strange little hut that stood on chicken-legs! And in that hut lived Baba Yaga, Grandmother Witch! One night the stepmother said to Vassilissa, "It's getting so dark, we must have more light! Tomorrow you must go to Baba Yaga and bring back a light." Vassilissa was so frightened, she didn't know what to do! But that night she took the little doll out of her apron pocket, and fed it a crust of bread that she had saved. When the doll was finished eating, Vassilissa said, "Little doll, what am I to do? My stepmother has sent me to Baba Yaga." The little doll said, "Don't worry, Vassilissa. Just get a good night's sleep, for the morning is wiser than the evening. And when you go to Baba Yaga, just be kind to everything you meet, and all will be well."

The next morning, Vassilissa took a bit of bread and a bit of meat and wrapped them up in a kerchief. Then with her doll in her apron pocket she set out for the house of Baba Yaga. When she got there, she saw it was a very curious sight! The house stood up on chicken-legs, and it could move to face this way or that! All around the house was a fence made of bones. As she neared the gate there was a dog that growled at her. "You poor thing!" said Vassilissa, when she saw how thin it was, and she reached into her pocket and gave it the crust of bread. So the dog just lay down and ate the bread. Nearer the gate, there was a cat who reached out its claws to scratch her face. But Vassilissa took the meat out of her pocket and gave it to the cat. So the cat just lay down and ate the meat. As she walked along the path to the hut, the heavy branches of a birch tree whipped out toward her face. She took her kerchief and tied back the branches. Then she looked up, and there was Baba Yaga! She was bony and thin, and her nose almost touched her chin, and her eyes seemed to burn like two coals!

"What do you want, my child?"

Vassilissa was so frightened that she could barely speak, but she curtsied and said, "Auntie, my stepmother sent me to fetch a light."

"Then just sit here at the loom and weave for me, and you shall have your light." And Vassilissa sat down at the loom and began to weave. After a while she looked down and saw that the cat was sitting there, looking at her.

"You are in danger," said the cat. "My mistress has gone to prepare a cooking pot, and when the water is boiling she is going to eat you!"

Vassilissa was almost frightened to death, but she said, "Please help me, little one! Tell me what to do!"

"Just let me weave in your place, and then you can run away," said the cat, and he changed places with Vassilissa.

"Are you weaving, my pretty?" called out Baba Yaga. And Vassilissa replied, "Yes, Auntie, I'm still weaving." Then she was about to leave when the cat said, "Take the towel and the comb from the table, and if you hear Baba Yaga coming close, throw them behind you, and they will help you. Then Vassilissa thanked the cat, took the towel and the comb, and ran out of the little house as fast as she could. When she came to the birch tree, the tree's branches were all tied up, so they didn't get in her way. When she went out the gate, the dog simply looked up at her, and then put his head on his paws and went back to sleep.

After a while Baba Yaga called out, "Are you still weaving, my sweet?" And the cat called out in a raspy voice, "Still weaving, Auntie." Of course, Baba Yaga knew it was not Vassilissa, and she came running into the little hut. "What!" she screamed at the cat. "Did you just let her run away? Why did you not scratch her eyes out?"

"All my life you have not given me so much as a kind word, but she fed me good meat!"

Baba Yaga gnashed her iron teeth and ran to the gate. "Why didn't you bite the girl?" she howled at the dog. "Why didn't you trip her up?" she asked the birch tree.

"You never gave me anything," said the dog, "but she fed me bread!"
"You never even trimmed me," said the tree, "but she gave me a beautiful kerchief!"

Baba Yaga climbed into her mortar and flew off, beating the way with her pestle, and sweeping away her tracks with a broom. After a time, Vassilissa could hear her getting closer and closer! So she threw the towel over her shoulder. Instantly there was a great river behind her! Baba Yaga had to stop. She got out of her mortar and began to drink. And she drank and drank until there wasn't a drop left. Then again she was chasing after Vassilissa. When Vassilissa heard her getting close, she threw the comb over her shoulder. Instantly a huge forest grew up behind her. Again, Baba Yaga had to stop. She began to gnaw away at that forest with her iron teeth, but the forest was too dense, and no matter how hard she tried, she couldn't get through it. So Vassilissa got away and ran home.

When she got home, her father was there, and when he found out what had happened, he drove the evil woman from the house, with her daughters. Vassilissa stayed with her father, and they prospered and lived together in health and happiness!

THE WORK:

This story gives one an opportunity to exercise all the research muscles because it is chock-full of traditional fairy-tale motifs which can be cross-referenced to variants from many different cultures. So I started with the Ashliman *Guide to Folktales in the English Language*. The primary Aarne-Thompson Tale Type is 313H, "Girl Escapes From a Witch." It's a compound story, so the other Tale Type is 480, "Kind and Unkind Girls." Then I went to MacDonald's *Sourcebook* to look up the principal motifs. The Baba Yaga story is classified like this: Q2.1.2 CeBb. That all breaks down to mean:

Q = Rewards and Punishments
  2. = Kind and Unkind
    .1 = (Kind and Unkind) *Girls*
      .2 = The Encounter en Route (sub-type)
        C = Pursuit Form
          eBb = Use of objects/obstacles (advice to hero or heroine from doll/mouse/other helper)

So, if we were to reduce the above notations to a couple of sentences, this story is about how a kind girl escapes from a witch with the magic help of her doll, some grateful animals (who reward her for her kindness), and several objects. The objects change to create obstacles that allow the girl to escape. In several stories that employ this device, a mirror is the object that turns into a body of water. Combs predominate as forests. In other pursuits, the pursuer and his or her prey change into different animals in order to swim lakes or fly through the air.

The doll is more than just a magical helper. It is a tangible connection to the dead mother and, as such, it is the protector of her child. Similar images include the bird who aids Aschenputtel. When *her* mother dies, a tree grows over the grave, and a beautiful bird comes to perch in the tree. It is this messenger from the spirit world who cares for the girl, provides her with three exquisite dresses, and exposes the deception with which the stepsisters attempt to win the Prince. In another Grimms' story, "The Juniper Tree" (#47), a bird is the spirit messenger from the little boy who is killed, cooked in a stew, and eaten by his own father! (This, by the way, is an example of a fascinating story that I would never tell to a child. I am not comfortable with my own feelings about the grisly events of the story.)

When I searched for variants, I was looking at both of the stories that I had merged, so I came up with the following: there is a story that is known as "The Gold in the Chimley." In it, a witch pursues two sisters. One girl was mean, stole a bag of gold from the witch, and refused to help several animals along the way. So, when the witch chases her, the animals refuse to shield the girl. The witch catches up with her and turns her into a stone! The second girl is kind to the animals she meets, so when the witch chases her, the animals say, no, they didn't see her, and the girl manages to escape. The animals are different from the ones in the Baba Yaga story, but the concept is the same.

Another variant is *Petronella*, by Jay Williams (Parents Magazine Press, 1978). In it, the kind and resourceful princess is advised by an old man to ask to serve the Enchanter and ask for certain objects in payment. When she is being pursued, Petronella throws those objects behind her, and they change into obstacles to slow down the Enchanter.

For other stories about sending a child into danger, there are a number of instances where a child is sent to find "the old woman of the forest." She is, of course, analogous to Baba Yaga. In the *Funk & Wagnalls Standard Dictionary of Folklore, Mythology, and Legend* there is additional information about her: "She is a guardian of the fountains of the water of life. . . . Her teeth and breasts of stone are used to tear her victims' flesh. She is often reduplicated in folktale, there being two or three sisters, all called Baba Yaga, all customarily lying in their huts, head to the door, a foot in either corner, and nose touching the ceiling." Well!

There is absolutely no description of a witch that compares with Baba Yaga. That is the one aspect of this tale which is totally Russian. And it is that quality of cultural identity that gives this tale its charm. There are negative aspects to this story for some people. The "Stepmother Issue" looms large, as does the abuse of a child. But I wanted to include this story, because it is rich with imagery, and it gives the storyteller something solid to research. In the original "Baba Yaga," when the little girl returns home, her father kills the stepmother and her daughters! In the original "Vassilissa the Beautiful," she is sent to her "auntie" in the forest to bring back some fire. Baba Yaga gives her a skull "with burning eyes." When Vassilissa returns home, the eyes glare at the stepmother and her daughters until it burns them up. Then Vassilissa buries the skull, and goes off to live with a childless old woman in the village, awaiting the return of her father. Eventually, with the help of her doll, she marries the Tsar.

In telling this story, I have a very straight-forward approach to describing Baba Yaga. I try to tell the "facts" about her appearance, her house, and her mode of transportation without editorializing. By that I mean that I don't dramatize or emphasize the spookiness of the story. The more you dwell on those details, the less impact they have on the listener. I try to picture those things while I am saying them, so that all of the gory elements have a real, sensory quality. The same rule holds true of the stepmother scenario, but for different reasons. I don't want to "comment" on the story when I tell it. When you hear tellers explaining or apologizing for the events in a story, it's a dead giveaway that the storyteller is uncomfortable. This story is an exercise in telling with a bold, confident style.

How the Camel Got His Hump (Kipling)

There has been so much discussion about how to treat literary tales that I wanted to include an example to show how one might work on them. There are certainly those who believe that the words of Kipling are sacred, and should not be altered for any reason! However, in a workshop that she did for the Storytelling Center, Inc. in New York City, storyteller, author, and teacher, Ellin Greene, gave the simplest and most eloquent description of how she approaches literary stories. "You have to tell them," she said, "so they *sound like the author's own words.*" Note that she didn't say one has to memorize the words, but she also didn't say you should "make it up as you go along." There is a particular style to an author's words, and to do justice to the story you must respect the rhythm, the sounds, the patterns and the choices.

The other factor to consider is that literary stories are just that—literary. They were crafted to be on paper, and when we choose to tell them to a group (as opposed to the one child who sits in your lap and looks at the pictures in the book) then we may have to be flexible with the language. The balance between complete, unquestioning faithfulness to the author's text, and "pandering" to an audience is a delicate one, and here is a demonstration of how I walk that tightrope.

The far left column has the story, exactly as Kipling wrote it. The center column is an exact transcription of what I say when I tell the story—including my introduction. The right-hand column gives a running description of what I do; facial gestures, body position, pauses, where they are important to the telling. I never "memorized" the story, but I believe that it still sounds like Kipling.

The Text:	*The Story:*	*The Moves:*
	Do you know how sometimes you wake up in the morning and you think, "I don't *wanna* get dressed! I don't *wanna* go to school! I don't *wanna* play with that toy! I don't *wanna* do ANY-THING!"? Do you ever feel like that? Do you know anyone *else* who is like that? Well, that's pretty lazy, isn't it? Well, another word for lazy	

The Text:	*The Story:*	*The Moves:*
	is "idle." Everyone say, "idle." (wait) That's right, idle. If you just want to sit around all day, then you are really . . . idle, that's right. If you were terribly, horribly, amazingly lazy, you could say you were (pause) "*'scrutiating* idle." Say that. (wait) Right. Well this is a story about the camel, who was 'scrutiating idle. Once, Oh Best Beloved, back when the world was so new and all, when the animals were just beginning to work for man, there was this *Camel,* and he lived in the middle of a howling desert, because he did *not want* to *work!* Uh-uh! (And besides, he was a howler himself!) So he ate sticks and thorns, tamarisk and milkweed, most 'scrutiating idle! And all he would ever say	By having the children say these words, I establish them as a "chorus."
Now this is the next tale, and it tells how the Camel got his big hump.		Take position in center of "stage." Mental breath. Begin.
In the beginning of years, when the world was so new-and-all, and the Animals were just beginning to work for Man, there was a Camel, and he lived in the middle of a Howling Desert because he did not want to work; and besides he was a Howler himself. So he ate sticks and thorns and tamarisks and milkweed and prickles, most 'scrutiating idle;		Emphasize <u>Camel</u>. "And besides . . . " deliver as an aside to audience at my right. <u>Chewing</u> — "sticks & thorns '"Humph!'" Camel face (grumpy, pouty, chew like a ruminant).

The Text:	*The Story:*	*The Moves:*

The Text:

and when anybody spoke to him he said "Humph!" Just "Humph!" and no more.

Presently the Horse came to him on Monday morning, with a saddle on his back and a bit in his mouth, and said, "Camel, O Camel, come out and trot like the rest of us."

"Humph!" said the Camel; and the Horse went away and told the Man.

Presently the Dog came to him, with a stick in his mouth, and said, "Camel, O Camel, come and fetch and carry like the rest of us."

"Humph!" said the Camel; and the Dog went away and told the Man.

Presently the Ox came to him, with the yoke on his neck, and said, "Camel, O Camel, come and

The Story:

was, "Humph!" Just "Humph!" and nothing more. Well, on the first day of the world—a Monday, I think it was—the Horse came to him with a saddle on his back, and a bit in his mouth, and the Horse said, "Camel, oh Camel, come on out and trot like the rest of us!" But the Camel just said, "Humph!" So the Horse went away, and he told . . . the Man. On the second day of the world the Dog came to him, with a stick in his mouth, and he said, "Camel, oh Camel, come on out and fetch and carry like the rest of us. But that Camel just looked at him and said, . . . "Humph!" So the Dog went away, and he told . . . the Man. On the third day the Ox

The Moves:

Touch back, point to mouth.

Position Camel to left, Horse to right.

"Camel (woof!), oh Camel (woof!)." Again, the Dog looks up and to the left, Camel looks down his nose and to the right.

The Text:	*The Story:*	*The Moves:*
plough like the rest of us."	came to him with a big heavy yoke across his neck for pulling things. And the Ox said, "Camel, oh Camel, come on out and plow like the rest of us." But that Camel just looked at him and	
"Humph!" said the Camel; and the Ox went away and told the Man.		*Ox speaks slower and deeper; "Camel, oooh, Camel . . ."*
At the end of the day the Man called the Horse and the Dog and the Ox together and said, "Three, O Three, I'm very sorry for you (with the world so new-and-all); but that Humph-thing in the Desert can't work, or he would have been here by now, so I'm going to leave him alone, and you must work double-time to make up for it."	said . . . "HUMPH!" So the Ox went away, and HE told . . . that's right. He told the Man. Well, at the end of the third day the Man called the Horse and the Dog and the Ox to him and said, "Three, oh Three, I'm sorry for you (what with the world so new and all), but that "humph" thing in the desert can't work, or he would have been here by now. So I'm going to	*Position the Man in center. "Gesture" to three (small hand gesture).*

Ox   Horse   Dog
Man

Man speaks to them.

That made the Three very angry (with the world so new-and-all), and they held a palaver, and an indaba, and a punchayet and a pow-wow on the edge of the Desert; and the Camel came, chewing	leave him alone. But *you* have to work double to make up for him!" Well, was that fair? ("no") Was	*"Well, was that . . . ?" to audience.*

The Text:

milkweed, most 'scru-
tiating idle, and
laughed at them.
Then he said,
"Humph!" and went
away again.

Presently there
came along the Djinn
in charge of All De-
serts, rolling in a
cloud of dust (Djinns
always travel that way
because it is magic),
and he stopped to
palaver and pow-wow
with the Three.

"Djinn of All De-
serts," said the
Horse, "is it right for
any one to be idle,
with the world so
new-and-all?"

"Certainly not,"
said the Djinn.

"Well," said the
Horse, "there's a
thing in the middle
of your Howling De-
sert (and he's a
Howler himself) with
a long neck and long
legs, and he hasn't
done a stroke of work
since Monday morn-
ing. He won't trot."

The Story:

that right? ("no!")
Well, it made the
Three very angry. So
they held a pow-wow.
And a palaver. And a
punchayet. And an
indaba. And a *CHAT*.
They held a meeting
on the edge of the
howling desert. And
the camel came
along, chewing on
thistles and prickles,
most 'scrutiating idle,
and he *laughed* at
them! "Ho ho ho!"
Then he just said,
"Humph!" and he
went away. Well,
presently, who should
come by but the
Djinni in charge of
all the deserts. He
came rolling in his
dust cloud. (Djinni's
always travel like
that, because it is
magic). And he
stopped to pow-wow
and palaver and chat
with the Three. And
the Horse said,
"Djinni in charge of
all the deserts, is it
right, what with the

The Moves:

Take chat to the
left. Camel comes
in R. Chewing
(between phrases.)

"Rolling" show with
hand gesture.

Horse shakes his
head/mane.

The Text:

"Whew!" said the Djinn, whistling, "that's my Camel, for all the gold in Arabia! What does he say about it?"

"He says 'Humph!'" said the Dog; "and he won't fetch and carry."

"Does he say anything else?"

"Only 'Humph!'.; and he won't plough," said the Ox.

"Very good," said the Djinn. "I'll humph him if you will kindly wait a minute."

The Djinn rolled himself up in his dustcloak, and took a bearing across the desert, and found the Camel most 'scrutiatingly idle, looking at his own reflection in a pool of water.

"My long and bubbling friend," said the Djinn, "what's this I hear of your doing no work, with the world so new-and-all?"

The Story:

world so new and all, for any animal not to work?" And the Djinni said, "No, that can't be right." "WELL," said the horse, "there's this *thing* in the middle of your howling desert (and he's a howler himself) with a long neck, and long legs, and he hasn't done a lick of work since Monday. He won't trot!" "Phew!" said the Djinni. "That's my Camel, for all the gold of Arabia. Does he have anything to say about it?" "He says 'Humph!'" said the Dog. "And he won't fetch and he won't carry!" "Does he say anything else?" "Only 'Humph!'" said the Ox, "and he won't plow!" "Very well," said the Djinni. "I'll just 'humph' him if you'll just wait a minute." And he rolled himself up in his dust cloud and set

The Moves:

"Well . . ." Stomp!

"Phew" W<u>hist</u>le (not word) Djinni talks to each animal — Position them.

"Rolled himself up" turn a circle and point — straight arm.

The Text:

"Humph!" said the Camel.

The Djinn sat down, with his chin in his hand, and began to think a Great Magic, while the Camel looked at his own reflection in the pool of water.

"You've given the Three extra work ever since Monday morning, all on account of your 'scrutiating idleness," said the Djinn; and he went on thinking Magics, with his chin in his hand.

"Humph!" said the Camel.

"I shouldn't say that again if I were you," said the Djinn; "you might say it once too often. Bubbles, I want you to work."

And the Camel said "Humph!" again; but no sooner had he said it than he saw his back, that he was so proud of, puffing up

The Story:

out across the desert to find the Camel. When he found him, the Camel was admiring his own reflection in a pool of water, chewing on thistles and prickles, tamarisk and milkweed, most 'scrutiating idle. "Well, my Long and Bubbling Friend. What's this I hear about your not doing any work?" The Camel just looked at him and said, . . . "Humph." The Djinni sat down, with his chin in his hand, and he began to think a great magic. "Let's see," he said. "Today's Thursday, and you've done no work at all since Monday, when the work began. You've missed three days, all on account of your 'scrutiating idleness. What do you have to say about it?" The Camel just looked at him and said, . . .

The Moves:

Camel looks over his right shoulder and down to water. Djinni bows (straight forward.)

Camel looks down his nose.

J balance on one foot, cross other leg over my knee, and "sit" with chin in hand.

Break pose.

The Text:

and puffing up into a great big lolloping humph.

"Do you see that?" said the Djinn. "That's your very own humph that you've brought on your very own self by not working. Today is Thursday, and you've done no work since Monday, when the work began. Now you are going to work."

"How can I," said the Camel, "with this humph on my back?"

"That's made a-purpose," said the Djinn, "all because you missed those three days. You will be able to work now for three days without eating, because you can live on your humph; and don't you ever say I never did anything for you. Come out of the Desert and go to the Three, and behave. Humph yourself!"

The Story:

"Humph!" "I wouldn't say that again, if I were you. You might find you'd said it once . . . too . . . often. Now, Bubbles, I want you to work!" But that Camel just looked at him and said, . . . "*HUMPH!*" But this time, when he did it, he saw his back, of which he'd been very proud, puffing up, and puffing up, and puffing up into one, great, big, huge, lolloping humph! "There!" said the Djinni. "Do you see that? That's your very own humph that you brought on your very own self, all because of your 'scruti-ating idleness. Now you are going to work!" "But how can I" said the Camel, "with this 'humph' thing on my back?" "Ah!" said the Djin, "that's made on pur-pose all on account of

The Moves:

Hands on hips. Talking faster up to the "H." ⎛This is the last "Humph!" Should be loudest.⎞

Gesture as if the humph was growing over my own shoulders/upper back.

Djinn smiles.

"But how can J . . . " This is the first time C speaks. J use a kind of stuffed nose "Duh" sound!

The Text:

And the Camel humphed himself, humph and all, and went to join the Three. And from that day to this the Camel always wears a humph (we call it "hump" now, not to hurt his feelings); but he has never yet caught up with the three days that he missed at the beginning of the world, and he has never yet learned how to behave.

The Story:

those three days that you missed at the beginning of the world. Now you can work for three days and three nights without ever stopping to eat. Because you can live on your 'humph'. Never say I didn't give you anything. *NOW*," said the Djinni, "I want you to go out of the desert, join the Three, and BEHAVE YOURSELF! HUMPH YOURSELF!" So the Camel humphed himself out of the desert, and he went to join the Three. And that's how the camel got that great big humph. Of course, we call it a hump, so we don't hurt his feelings. But you know, that Camel never made up for the three days that he missed at the beginning of the world, and he has never learned how to behave himself!.

The Moves:

"Now . . . " change pace. Number the three items:
1. go out of desert
2. join 3
3. BEHAVE!
CLAP HANDS!
"Humph yourself" when C "humphs," J do a rolling step, only 2 or 3 beats.

Last sentence — Definitive!!

Some additional notes on this story: In telling any story in which the language is not current, you have to make choices about what to change and how to change it. Too many changes destroy the character and the flow of the speech, but on the other hand you want children to be able to follow the path of the story without too much trouble. After all, these Kipling stories were first published in 1902. Some words can be explained if you can do it quickly and not too didactically. Since I usually tell this story to my youngest audiences, I explain the concept of " 'scrutiating idle," but I don't bother to explain the grammar! After all, it makes no difference to the enjoyment of the story—could even be detrimental to enjoying it—to learn the word "excrutiatingly." Some words can be left a mystery. It's fun to allow your audience the luxury of their own definitions for words like "punchayet" . . . as long as you give them enough clues to make sense out of the sentence. So I chose to leave some of the foreign and arcane words, and just add "chat" (or sometimes, "meeting") to the phrase. The spatial references and voice indicators in the third column can also serve to help you eliminate lots of "he said, she said." But you have to be very clear and unfussy in order to do that. I made simple, distinct choices for phrasing certain passages, and I am consistent throughout the story. This helps make the audience feel comfortable joining in, because I give the same cues each time I want a certain response. So the cues for "humph" are different than those for " 'scrutiating idle." Also, I give time in the phrasing for the children to respond, but if they don't—or if their responses are too slow, so they violate the internal rhythm of the words—I don't pause longer than a second or two. By the second cue, the children fit their "lines" into the speech patterns I've set up, and they—the children—become a chorus, an integral part of the story.

It might be tempting to try to look at this and the other tales in *Just So Stories* from the perspective of British imperialism in India. It would probably be a mistake to try to find the potent, hidden, psychological meanings in this story. It would be disastrous to analyze Kipling's historical paradigm. I think I speak for most teachers, storytellers, and children when I say, please don't! If you are tempted to try, perhaps storytelling isn't your game! This is a story to relish for the fun and the sound and the silliness of it. The "work ethic" message is obviously secondary to the word-play.

CHAPTER 10

Final Thoughts

> The knowledge that one is to be hanged at dawn focuses the mind
> wonderfully!
>
> Sir Alec Guinness in *Kind Hearts and Coronets.*

It is in the nature of every project that one could go on and on, fixing and adding and tinkering, until finally there was nothing left of the original impulse, the initiating idea. My hope was that, by setting down *my* processes, I could encourage the reader to pursue, seriously and playfully, his or her own process of inquiry into this most engaging, intriguing, life-affirming art form! On the other hand, I never meant to imply that anyone should spend years researching a million variants and all their tale types, motifs, and cultural implications before telling them! Only in the act of telling can we learn the truth about these, or any stories. That truth is highly subjective, and changes with each teller and with each group of listeners.

It's important to realize that the only person who can give you directions on how to tell a story is you. No one has a lock on the "right" way to tell any particular story, no matter how strongly they feel about it. The other thing to realize is that stories in general—and powerful ones, like fairy tales, in particular—can provoke very strong emotions in the tellers and the listeners. That's probably why I am drawn to fairy tales: They have a hint of danger about them, both inherently and in the act of telling them. It's a little like dancing on a tightrope. And all the study and preparation in the world won't make these stories ordinary! If you are drawn to them at all, then you will never tire of them.

PART III

Resources

Sources for Story References in Part I

These are some sources for stories that are cited or referred to in the first eight chapters of this book. You can undoubtedly find most of these stories in other collections, in addition to those listed below. All Grimms' stories are identified by the number assigned to them in any collection of the complete fairy tales of the Brothers Grimm.

Chapter 1

"Urashima" (Japanese) in *Best Loved Folktales of the World*, ed. by Joanna Cole. New York: Anchor Press, 1983. Also found in *Favorite Folktales from around the World*, ed. by Jane Yolen. New York: Pantheon, 1986.

"Rip Van Winkle" from *The Sketch Book*, by Washington Irving, 1820. In *The Legend of Sleepy Hollow and Other Selections from Washington Irving*, ed. by Austin McC. Fox. New York: Washington Square Press, 1962.

Just So Stories by Rudyard Kipling. New York: Macmillan, 1902. Reprinted by Viking Penguin, 1989. First published by Macmillan, 1902. These stories were originally published individually, the first, "How the Whale Got His Throat," in 1897, in *St. Nicholas Magazine*.

Chapter 4

"Donkey Skin" by Charles Perrault, circa 1690. Available in various collections, including *The Fairy Tales of Charles Perrault*, ed. by Angela Carter. New York: Avon Books, 1979. (Tale Type 510B *King Tries to Marry His Own Daughter.*)

"The Girl Who Banished Seven Youths" in *Arab Folktales*, tr. and ed. by Inea Bushnaq. New York: Pantheon, 1986.

"Maid Maleen" by the Brothers Grimm, tale #198. (Tale Type 870 *The Entombed Princess.*)

"East of the Sun and West of the Moon" (Norway) in *Best Loved Folktales of the World*, ed. by Joanna Cole. New York: Anchor Press, 1983. Also in *One Hundred Favorite Folktales*, coll. by Stith Thompson. Bloomington, IN.: Indiana University Pr., 1968. (Tale Type 425A *The Animal Bridegroom.*)

"The Black Bull of Norroway" in *The Blue Fairy Book*, ed. by Andrew Lang. Mineola, NY: Dover Publications, 1965. (Tale Type 425A *The Animal Bridegroom.*)

"White Bear Whittington" in *Who Blowed Up the Church House? and Other Ozark Folk Tales* by Vance Randolph. New York: Columbia Univ. Pr., 1952. (Tale Type 425A *The Animal Bridegroom.*)

"Hans My Hedgehog" by the Brothers Grimm, tale #108. (Tale Type 441 *The Animal Offspring.*)

Chapter 5

"Petronella" in *The Practical Princess and Other Liberating Fairy Tales* by Jay Williams. New York: Parents Magazine Press, 1978.

"Cinderella" by the Brothers Grimm, tale #21. (Tale Type 510A.)

"Spindle, Shuttle, and Needle" by the Brothers Grimm, tale #188. (Tale Type 585.)

"Mossycoat" in *Folktales of England*, ed. by Katherine M. Briggs. Chicago: Chicago Univ. Pr., 1965. Similar versions of this story are known as "Cap O'Rushes," "Tattercoat," "Donkey Skin," and many other titles.

Chapter 6

"Rapunzel" by the Brothers Grimm, tale #12. (Tale Type 310 *The Maiden in the Tower.*)

"The Little Sea Hare" by the Brothers Grimm, tale #191. (Tale Type 554 *The Grateful Animals.*)

Chapter 8

"The Song of Gimmile" in *The King's Drum* by Harold Courlander. New York: Voyager Books, Harcourt, Brace & World, 1962.

Cinderella variants:

"Cinderella" by Charles Perrault

"Ashenputtel" by the Brothers Grimm

"The Indian Cinderella" in *Canadian Wonder Tales* by Cyrus Macmillan. London and Toronto: Bodley Head, 1974. Also in *North American Legends*, ed. by Virginia Hamilton. Illus. by Ann Strugnell. New York: Collins, 1979. The title of this story incorrectly implies that there is one American Indian Cinderella story. In fact, in Virginia Hamilton's collection, there is the Zuni story, "Poor Turkey Girl," that is yet another Cinderella-type story.

APPENDIX B

Sources for Story Texts in Part II

"The Twelve Huntsmen" by the Brothers Grimm, tale #67. (Tale Type 84 *The Forsaken Fiancee*.) I have used the following sources to shape the version I tell:

The Juniper Tree and Other Tales from Grimm, tr. by Lore Segal and Randall Jarrell. Pictures by Maurice Sendak. New York: McGraw-Hill, 1976 (pap).

The Complete Grimm's Fairy Tales, by Jacob Grimm and Wilhelm K. Grimm. Tr. by Margaret Hunt, rev. by James Stern. New York: Random House, 1972.

"The Sack of Truth," adapted from the version collected by Ruth Sawyer. In *Picture Tales from Spain*, originally published by F. A. Stokes, 1936. I found it in *A Child's Treasury of Fairy Tales and Legends*, edited by Alice Schneider, illustrated by Erika Weihs. New York: Grosset and Dunlap, 1946.

"The Silent Princess," adapted from "The Mute Princess" in the collection *Elijah's Violin*, ed. by Howard Schwartz. New York: Harper & Row, 1985. Additional influences on this version of the tale include other riddle stories, and "The Princess Who Refused to Talk" in *Jewish Folktales*, selected and retold by Pinhas Sader. New York: Doubleday, 1989.

"Dorani," in *The Olive Fairy Book*, ed. by Andrew Lang. London: Longmans, Green, and Co., Ltd., 1907. Dover Reprint, 1967.

"The Grateful Crane." There are numerous retellings of this Japanese story, both in collections and in picture books. A few notable versions are:

> *The Story of the Grateful Crane* by Jennifer Bertoli. Illustrated under the direction of Kozo Shimizumi. Morton Grove, IL: Albert Whitman, 1977.
>
> "The Cloth of a Thousand Feathers" from *Men from the Village Deep in the Mountains and Other Japanese Folk Tales* by Garrett Bang. New York: Macmillan, 1979.
>
> *Japanese Children's Stories* by Florence Sakade. Illustrated by Yoshio Hayashi. Rutland, Vt.: Charles E. Tuttle, 1958.

"How the Camel Got His Hump" in *Just So Stories,* by Rudyard Kipling. New York: Macmillan, 1902. Reprint by Penguin, 1989.

"Vassilissa and Baba Yaga." The following sources were used in creating this story:

> *Russian Fairy Tales*, coll. by Aleksandr Afanas'ev, tr. by Norbert Guterman. New York: Pantheon, 1945. ("Baba Yaga," page 194; "Baba Yaga," page 363; "Vassilissa the Beautiful," page 439.) See also, if you can locate it, the large-format paperback version of *Vassilissa the Beautiful*, printed in the U.S.S.R. in 1976, for its stunning and evocative illustrations.

I. Library Resources

Aarne, Antti, and Stith Thompson. *The Types of Folktales: A Classification and Bibliography.* Folklore Fellows Communications, no. 184. Helsinki: Suomalainen Tiedeakatemia, 1973.

Ashliman, D. L. *A Guide to Folktales in the English Language.* Westport, Ct.: Greenwood Press, 1987.

Leach, Maria, ed. *Funk & Wagnalls Standard Dictionary of Folklore, Mythology, and Legend.* New York: Harper & Row, 1984. (pap.)

MacDonald, Margaret Read. *The Storyteller's Sourcebook: A Subject, Title, and Motif Index to Folklore Collections for Children.* Detroit: Neal-Schuman/Gale Research, 1982.

Fowler, H. W., and F. G. Fowler, eds. *The Concise Oxford English Dictionary.* Clarendon: Oxford Univ. Pr., 1929. The concise edition and the abridged two-volume set are both fine. If you prefer to buy your own edition, mail-order book clubs sometimes offer them fairly inexpensively.

Nonprint:

The American Storytelling Series. Bronx: H. W. Wilson, 1986. Especially the following video tapes: Volume 2, "White Wave" (Diane Wolkstein); Volume 3, "The Woodcutter" (Laura Simms); Volume 4, "Grass Cape" (Jon Spelman); Volume 6, "Hansel and Gretel" (Ed Stivender); Volume 7, "The Twelve Huntsmen" (Marcia Lane). There is also a literary fairy tale on Volume 1 in this series, "How the Whale Got His Throat" by Kipling, told by Jackson Gillman, and an updated fairy tale on Volume 5, "Cindy Ellie," told by Mary Carter Smith. All in all, this video series gives you a feeling for the range of possible style and presentation choices.

II. Home Resource Collection

These are standard reference works that you would probably want to own:

A good dictionary. (See suggestion above. But, while the O.E.D. is terrific, many other standards are just fine.)

Roget's International Thesaurus. Fourth Edition. Revised by Robert L. Chapman. New York: Harper & Row, 1977.

Shedlock, Marie L. *The Art of Storytelling.* New York: Dover Publications, 1951.
This was originally published in 1915, and some of the "rules" may seem quaint and old-fashioned. However, much of what was true then still holds true, and this was the very first book about storytelling I ever read.

The following books are my own favorite fairy-tale/folktale commentaries. They were instrumental in the writing of this book, and I have quoted from them liberally:

Cook, Elizabeth. *The Ordinary and the Fabulous.* 2nd ed. with addendum. New York: Cambridge Univ. Pr., 1978.

Cooper, J. C. *Fairy Tales: Allegories of the Inner Life.* Wellingborough, Northamptonshire: Aquarian Press, 1983. (pap.)

Dorson, Richard M., ed. *Folklore and Folklife.* Chicago: University of Chicago Press, 1972.
Especially fine is Linda Degh's chapter on folk narrative.

Douglas, Mary. *Implicit Meanings.* London: Routledge & Kegan Paul, 1978. (pap.)

Lüthi, Max. *Once Upon a Time: On the Nature of Fairy Tales.* Tr. by Lee Chadeayne and Paul Gottwald. Induction and reference notes by Francis Lee Utley. Bloomington: Indiana Univ. Pr., 1976. (pap.)

_____. *The European Folktale: Form and Nature.* Tr. by John D. Niles. Bloomington: Indiana Univ. Pr., 1986. (pap.)

_____. *The Fairytale as Art Form and Portrait of Man.* Tr. by Jon Erickson. Bloomington: Indiana Univ. Pr., 1984. (pap.)
Sometimes, you find a writer who makes sense to you, and is also surprising and exciting. Lüthi confirms my instincts and informs my guesses.

Pellowski, Anne. *The World of Storytelling.* Bronx: H. W. Wilson, 1990.

Tatar, Maria. *The Hard Facts of the Grimms' Fairy Tales.* Princeton: Princeton Univ. Pr., 1987. (pap.)

III. Story Collections

The greatest danger for a student of storytelling is to develop a taste for picture books! They are beautiful, but also expensive, and with only one story per volume, it takes a lot of shelf space to accumulate a decent-sized story collection. Besides, larger volumes frequently contain useful notes on background and origin, as well as bibliographies. Here is a "starter list" of folk/fairy tale collections that should keep anyone busy for many years.

Clarkson, Atelia, and Gilbert B. Cross. *World Folktales: A Scribner Resource Collection.* New York: Charles Scribner's Sons, 1980. (pap.)

As noted elsewhere in this book, this is both a collection of stories and a research tool.

Thompson, Stith, ed. *One Hundred Favorite Folktales.* Bloomington: Indiana Univ. Pr., 1968. (pap.)

This is a collection of well-known European stories, arranged in tale-type numerical order with notes on sources for each tale.

The "Color" Fairy Books by Andrew Lang. There are twelve of these (blue, red, yellow, pink, violet, crimson, orange, grey, olive, brown, lilac, and green), chockful of stories from a variety of literary and oral nineteenth-century sources. All are published by Dover Publications, New York. The illustrations by H. J. Ford are as "classic" as the stories themselves. Originally published by Longmans, Green, and Co., Inc. from 1889 (circa) to 1909.

The Complete Fairy Tales of the Brothers Grimm. There are several different translations to choose from, including the Bantam edition with an introduction by Jack Zipes, and the Pantheon edition with an introduction by Padraic Colum and commentary by Joseph Campbell. You need to own one and be cognizant of the others, as different translations yield different information.

Pantheon has created a wonderful series of folktales from many different cultures and countries. A few examples are: *African Folktales, Chinese Fairy Tales and Fantasies, Italian Folktales, Yiddish Folktales, French Folktales, Russian Fairy Tales, Victorian Fairy Tales.* The list is long and is growing every year. Quantity and quality of the notes vary from volume to volume, but sources are usually given, and each collection contains an extensive bibliography. One can only hope that the people at Pantheon never stop!

Another excellent folk- and fairy-tale series is published by the University of Chicago Press. The series is edited by folklorist Richard M. Dorson, and it includes excellent notes on the types and motifs of each story. The books are called *Folktales of* . . . (Egypt, England, Chile, Hungary, etc.), with more than a dozen titles at last count.

Literary Folk Tales

These are my personal favorites. Some of the authors whose stories move and delight me are:

Babbit, Natalie. *The Devil's Storybook*. (New York: Farrar, Straus & Giroux, 1984) and *The Devil's Other Storybook*, (New York: Farrar, Straus & Giroux, 1987). Funny and magical.

Farjeon, Eleanor. *The Little Bookroom*. (Boston: David R. Godine, 1984, pap.) and *The Old Nurse's Stocking Basket* (Silver Spring, Md.: Henry Z. Walck, Inc., 1965).

These are my favorites among this author's numerous collections of wonderful stories.

Pyle, Howard. *The Wonder Clock*. New York: Dover, 1965.

Fairy tales so true to older, oral tales that they don't "feel" literary.

Singer, Isaac Bashevis. *When Shlemeil Went to Warsaw and Other Stories*. New York: Farrar, Straus & Giroux, 1986.

Look for the many collections of his other Jewish stories, too, including one with "Zlateh the Goat." Originally written in Yiddish, they abound with imps and *lantuchs* and other strange creatures. Singer combined the folklore he heard as a child with his own, brilliantly original, plots and details.

Yolen, Jane. *The Girl Who Cried Flowers and Other Tales*. New York: Crowell Jr. Books, 1974, pap.; *The Moon Ribbon and Other Tales*. New York: Thomas Y. Crowell, 1976 (op); *The Hundredth Dove*. New York: HarperCollins, 1987); and *The Dream Weaver*. New York: Putnam, 1989.

Look for these and many other collections of Yolen's wonderful, magical fairy tales.